Paper Trails

Comment and Context
Place . . . Time . . . Meaning

Graham Hutchins

VANTAGE PRESS
New York

Published by Vantage Press, Inc.
419 Park Avenue South, New York, NY 10016

Manufactured in the United States of America
ISBN: 978-0-533-16142-3
Library of Congress Catalog Card No.: 2008908675

0 9 8 7 6 5 4 3 2 1

To my *Paper Trails People* throughout the world who allowed me to share these thoughts via e-mail over the last few months and years, and encouraged me to publish them in a book.

Contents

Paper Trails

Sent: Tuesday, January 27, 2004 2:29 P.M.

Subject: *Paper Trails*
Greetings . . .

In the process of gathering together my various ramblings or writings I have an urge to share them again. It occurred to me that I have kept notebooks and journals over the years in which I collected them, mostly named for places in which I lived and studied or served the church and taught. It all began with my *Edinburgh Papers,* a journal I kept when while a student there. There followed the *Monitor Papers,* the *Vancouver Papers,* the *Ferndale Papers,* the *Palouse Papers,* the *Port Angeles Papers,* and the *Jakarta Journal* and *La Paz Papers.* Then came the *9/11 Papers.* In going through them guess what! I hit on the idea to call the collection *Paper Trails* . . . isn't that original?! Some of you have seen some of these before in newsletter articles, on emails, or heard some of them in sermons, or in my poems. Anyway, I am sending some of them out from time to time, edited a little perhaps, and briefly presented to distract you from the frenzy of our modern world and its wars and politics and nonsense. So, from time to time, try a quick read for a few moments. They won't necessarily be in the order of their initial writing. I hope you enjoy them. It will keep me at the discipline of gathering and refining them, and out of other kinds of trouble! As Karl Barth said in the preface of one of his volumes of Theology . . . "while having still time on the earth."

I got this idea the other day while baking some bread. Which brought to mind the following reflections I had a few years ago.

On Bread and Basics

I baked some bread again today. There is something basic about bread . . . and the baking of it. Something elemental and substantial. It reminded me of how several years ago I baked some "Parson's Bread" and "Preacher Loaf" for the bazaar in one of my congregations. Not bad bread [under Dory's watchful eye] for a newcomer to such a basic industry! I've baked quite a few loaves since, though not lately. But today, on the birthday observance of one of our century's Christian martyrs, Dr. Martin Luther King, I baked some bread.

Just the ingredients the recipe called for gave rise [no pun intended] to some reflections that spoke to me of other basics:

Flour—certainly there would be no bread without flour. But flour itself comes from elsewhere, from wheat or some other grain. Is everything the gifted result of something else? Are we? To each other?

Milk—Isn't there a word about "human kindness" in relation to this? What would our lives be without the warm nurture of milk? Or cool refreshing kindness?

Salt—Aha! Now we are really getting biblical! Seasoning and zest, preservation and flavor. We are called to be that! Salt that disappears but enlivens the world and keeps it from going flat! "You"—Jesus said, "are the salt of the earth!"

Butter—Ah! Such richness that brings the golden crust to life. Bread without crust is like a sandwich without a filling! Should not we be the crusty Christians? And present a warm and glowing countenance to the world?

Cracked wheat—Here is not just the heart of the grain, but the husk as well. The whole grain is offered! I think of another Christian martyr . . . a bishop of the ancient church, who said on his way to Rome to be put to death, that he was "God's wheat," glad to be broken and ground to flour for Christ.

Sunflower seeds—for delight and taste and texture. From an amazing plant that follows the risen Sun wherever it goes. Our "Sun" has risen too, and if we keep our faces turned toward him we ourselves will bring delight and texture to the world.

Honey—This is added to bring sweet witness to the bread and to our own life and witness. May the word of Christ be to us "sweeter than the honeycomb!"

Water—even more basic to life than flour. We are born in it, and born in it again in our baptism. It brings life to the world, and combines the other ingredients of life's recipes into a unity of purpose and relationship.

Yeast—the source of the inner transformation that explodes the water combined ingredients into the fulfillment of their harmony through a dance of kneading and pounding and waiting and rising and watching and baking into a glorious presentation of fragrance and beauty and texture and life!

No wonder Jesus took bread and said, "This is my body."
"O taste and see that the Lord is good!"

—from "The View from the Tower"—*The Tower Echoes*, 1st United Methodist and Congregational Church, Port Angeles, Washington.

The Palouse Papers

Consider the Heavens

By Graham Hutchins—Simpson United Methodist Church

We had fallen asleep in the hammock as the sun went down, lulled to slumber by the gentle breeze from the nearby sea.

I awoke to the sound of an airplane and sat up. The jet engines roared almost gently as the airliner gained altitude, its lights announcing its path across the dark shadow of the great mountain.

Behind and just above the mountain's crest a full moon had risen, flooding the world with a soft but radiant light. The moonlight filtered through the banyan tree and made patterns on the lawn, turned the sea to silver, and transformed the surf to a shimmering necklace on the shore.

Not far from the shining moon, the great evening star hung in the southern sky, adding its own light to the already luminous evening. It was a time for wonder and reflection, and the enjoyment of just experiencing the beauty of it all.

Then the lights of the airplane, the rising moon, and the brilliant evening star led me to ponder the appearance of it all in a new way.

It was the plane that had awakened me to this scene. I did not hear the moon rise, or see the evening star. And now the plane was gone, moving swiftly on its journey to who knows where.

The moon and the evening star hardly seemed to move at all. And yet I knew that tiny plane could never keep up with the moon in its orbit around the earth, or with the evening star [the planet Venus?] in its orbit around the sun.

The night around me was bathed in the mysterious light of the full moon, which seemed to be the greatest light in the evening sky, and yet I knew that the planet rising beside it could outshine it by far, and no doubt had its own moons that might dwarf the one that filled my world with radiance. And that our moon and the distant planet were themselves, like earth, but reflectors of the light of the sun. And that beyond the giant planet hanging in the sky the tiny stars were themselves suns, that gave their light to worlds of their own, that might have their own moons . . . and perhaps someone sitting beside some starlit sea filled with wonder at the thousand eyes of night.

How relative things are! How important to realize that we see from where we are, and always in that perspective. How true it is that "now we know in part."

Before my very eyes, the brightest object was really the dimmest, the swiftest the slowest, the largest the smallest. The great mountain that filled the eastern horizon would be a pimple on the face of the moon. The moon would be a tiny satellite to the giant planet that looked so small beside it. The planet would be like a tiny satellite to the distant stars, as it is to our own star, the sun. The roar of the jet engines that disturbed my sleep would hardly be a whisper in the vast silence of space.

And what of me, my wife that sleeps beside me, and all our human kind and kin; who on moonlit nights, like some ancient Psalmist, consider the heavens, the moon and the stars? And wonder also, what our place is in this immensity.

We wonder much, and know in part [and come to comprehend how little we really know]; and yet are moved to trust that behind, beyond, and within this vast array of night and light, we too, are known and seen and held in light. And that we are privileged to wear this knowledge like a crown, and know it is our glory.

Today's Thought—Keolahoe Community Church, Kihei, Maui, Hawaii—*The Pullman Herald*, September 6, 1986, Pullman, Washington.

The Port Angeles Papers

The Bookstore Blues—Or Is It Cheers?!

On my study wall is a print of an elderly white-haired gentleman standing on top of a stepladder in a huge library. He has in one hand an open book, holds another to his face, a volume is tucked under his arm, and yet one more between his legs. Dangling from the pocket of his greatcoat is a long white rag for the purpose of dusting the shelves. Lost in his reading and with a look of curious wonder on his face, he has entirely forgotten why he climbed the ladder. The painting, in a Vienna gallery, is aptly called *The Bookworm*.

Recently, downtown for an appointment that didn't last long, I headed for the Family Shoe Store sale. On the way I came to the Odyssey Bookshop and fell right in! I love books! I also have too many of them and don't need any more, but keep buying them anyway! In Ecclesiastes we read: "Of the making of many books there is no end, and of much study a weariness of the flesh." The writer could well have said "of the *buying* of many books there is no end!"

Knowing all this, I entered anyway and spent a few minutes

browsing among the shelves. At such times a dialogue goes on in my head, e.g., "Hutchins, why are you in this place?" Answer: "Obviously I'm looking at books!" "But you don't need any more books!" "Yes, but this one here . . . is really the latest . . . the best . . . the . . ." "But you should read the books you already have!" And so it goes . . . as I try to talk myself out of buying more.

Two of my favorite authors recently wrote about the joy and importance of summer reading—and the books they put aside during the rest of the year to read during the "break." The problem with most of us is that we either don't take the time to read or don't have it. For someone like me, whose life is in the "Word" this can be a very dangerous evasion. One must, after all, prime the pump to irrigate the fields. I must read therefore—not just the Word—but many words about the Word, and other words about a lot of things. But when I survey the horizon of volumes that lies before me on my shelves, in a bookstore or a library, I despair of ever reading them all! Then I go and buy more! I am a bookworm!

Stephen Spender has a great little poem that applies here . . .

I saw a man pursuing the horizon.
On and on he sped. "But you can never . . ." I said.
"You lie!" he cried, and ran on.

I sometimes think I am like that man. Perhaps we all are. We long for "world enough and time" to read all we need or want to read, and the horizon just recedes before us running to catch it! No wonder we need new shoes! Such is the human condition.

Thoughts like these could give you the blues in the bookstore! But perhaps we should be of good cheer and grateful we can read at all—so many people can't—even if they had the time. One of the greatest achievements of the Christian Church is that its joy in the Word of God has led it to translate that Word into the words of every language, tribe and tongue so that all everywhere might learn to "read and inwardly digest" the good news from God.

So read on! Through summer and into the autumn of your days!
On! On to the horizon!

The irony of all this is that I came home and wrote about it! More words! Hope you had time to read them!

—The View from the Tower—1996.

The Palouse Papers and The Port Angeles Papers

The Cathedral of Gloom

If I say, Let only darkness cover me, and the night about me be light, even the darkness is not dark to you, the light is as bright as the day; for darkness is as light with you.

—Psalms 139:11-12.

We approached the mouth of the cave and looked inside. It appeared to be a vast cavern that we estimated might hold over a thousand people. Seeing no one within, we hesitated to step into the gloomy interior. It attracted us with curiosity and yet seemed foreboding and mysterious.

At our backs was the late afternoon sun on the azure sea, and the rhythmic pounding of the surf. Before us was this gigantic hole in the mountainside that gathered gloom and darkness; the further one traveled from that shining sea.

The floor of the cavern was of sand, and seemed a kind of beach on the shore of a vast ocean of darkness. As our eyes grew accustomed to the diminishing light we made our way further into this overwhelming mystery.

Suddenly we discovered we were not alone! Ahead of us we heard voices, and then realized that they were children's voices! Laughing voices of children at play! It was a sound one would expect to hear in the familiar vicinity of a backyard playground, but hardly in that great and gloomy silence. Indeed, it was utterly incongruous!

We traversed a small rise on that subterranean beach and found indeed some children on the other side of it running and shouting as if in broad daylight under a friendly sky. Why did they seem so at home in that awesome place?

Their voices were glad expressions of delight, not the careful murmurs of foreboding, to say nothing of the cries of children afraid of the dark. They were totally at ease, and even boisterous . . . where hushed whispers seemed the only appropriate response in this cathedral of gloom.

Then we noticed what made the difference—*their father* was with them! Under his watchful but gentle eye, and within the orbit of his love and presence, they felt secure and free to explore and romp and play as if in their own backyard.

A place of gloom was transformed into a place of glee. The forbidding dark was filled with bright laughter. The dim and mysterious cavern was something to explore not something to fear. Secure in the caring presence of a parent's love they found this new environment a welcome and exciting place to be.

Is there a parable here?

Do we confront gloomy caverns of the heart? Despair, guilt, grief—or the anxious foreboding of a world that seems to stumble blindly into a "heart of darkness?" Our world, our community, our families, even our own lives can be weighed down with problems and overshadowed with gloom. Life can seem more like a cave every day. Or a bottomless pit.

Do we hear the voices of children at play? Perhaps they perceive something we forgot to notice?

Maybe we need to "become as little children" again, and realize that we are not alone.

As we follow Jesus in this Lenten journey to the cross where he trusted the One he called "Father" even in the gathering darkness of his mission, let us also learn to trust and come to understand that with God—*the night is as bright as the day, and the darkness is as the light.*

Thought for the Day—*The Pullman Herald*, September 3, 1986, "The Cathedral of Gloom," "View from the Tower"—*Tower Echoes*, First United Methodist and Congregational Church, Port Angeles, Washington.

A Tale of Two Frogs

We went early to the pool one morning. After a refreshing dip and a brief swim, Dory noticed something clinging to the opposite edge of the pool. We swam over to look . . . and were confronted with one of the most amazing things we have ever experienced.

It was a frog . . . as we surmised . . . not just one frog . . . but two! We almost backed away in embarrassment at interfering in a bit of private froggy procreation! But then we noticed something else was going on here. A large brown frog had a smaller one on its back clinging with its arms to it like a child to its mother. Then Dory noticed that the bigger frog was missing a hind leg, and had only a stump there, as though it had gotten away from an attacker or a trap of some sort. The smaller frog . . . clinging to the back of the bigger frog had all its limbs but was firmly holding on to the big frog and would not let go.

They went back into the water of the pool, and we suddenly noticed that the little frog was helping the big frog swim! It would swim with both its hind feet, while the big frog swam with its one remaining hind leg . . . and in perfect coordination! The big frog then climbed out of the pool . . . [the little frog was of no help here] and then when they made their way along the edge of the pool, the little frog helped the big one to walk! But this time with only *one* leg . . . the left leg of the little frog walking in coordination with the big right leg of the larger frog! It was an amazing sight!

They stayed out of the pool a short while and then went in again, then out again . . . and back and forth. I meanwhile ran back to our apartment to get the cameras . . . and we have some incredible video and pictures of these two . . . who seemed to demonstrate intelligence, compassion, cooperation, and coordination to an incredible degree! The big frog had a real struggle getting out of the pool, and would often fall back on the steel bar just under the surface of the water to "get a run at it" and sometimes that would work. But then . . . after a few tries . . . it did something that again showed intelligent planning. It made its way, with its passenger still clinging to its back . . . along the edge of the pool to the corner where the two could get leverage on the right angle of the ledge and crawl out much easier! We were astounded!

The last we saw of them . . . they were making their way along the side of the pool toward the garden . . . and just then the great fish fountains at the end of the pool came on with those wonderful streams of water gushing out of their mouths, almost as if to celebrate the successful morning dip of the incredible caring frogs!

Is there a lesson here? We have often heard of "nature, red in tooth and claw" and have seen some astonishing films on television to make the point. And yet, is there not another side to it? How about nature's nurturing, caring, and marvelous symphony of life? The evening news all too often displays all around us how it is that we humans are still in what the philosopher Thomas Hobbes called the "state of nature" where "life is solitary, mean, nasty, dirty, brutish and short." A "war of each against all," and of "every man against every man." Maybe we need to see that the "brutes" . . . on the other hand can sometimes teach us caring, compassion, and even something we call love.

We, who call ourselves Christians, follow One who taught us to consider the lilies, and the birds of the air, and likened God to a mother hen watching over her brood. If He had come by the pool where we were that morning, we are sure He would have also said . . . "Consider these frogs . . . and learn from them . . . how to care for one another!"

—Jakarta, Indonesia, Transfiguration, 2000.

Lest We Forget

If then the light in you is darkness, how great is the darkness!

—Matthew 6:23

I met her in Heathrow Airport in London. She was waiting for a flight to Montreal as I was waiting for one to Seattle. I had just arrived from Edinburgh. She had flown in from Johannesburg. We struck up a conversation, and I asked how she liked living in South Africa. She liked it very much, she said, and told how it was a great place to live and work and that she really wouldn't want to live anywhere else.

Thinking of the tense racial unrest in South Africa at that time due to apartheid, I ventured to ask, "Doesn't the political situation down there bother you?"

"Oh, I'm not interested in politics," she said. "I find all that rather boring." The conversation went on as she told me about her work and her interests.

Finally, feeling somewhat bold again, I said, "How could you not be interested in politics down there? Aren't you afraid of suddenly waking up one day to a frightful situation, with blood running in the streets and all of that?"

"No, not at all," she replied. "I never think of those kinds of things."

"But don't you suppose," I went on, "there were a lot of people in Germany in the thirties that 'never thought about politics' and suddenly found themselves in a horrible . . ."

I didn't get to finish my sentence, as she said, "Oh yes, my parents had to flee from Germany to Canada in the late thirties. That's who I am going to see in Montreal. And, oh . . . excuse me . . . now they are calling my flight. . . . Goodbye."

As I watched her exit through the departure lounge door, I sadly reflected on Santayana's saying regarding those who do not learn from history . . . and how they are probably destined to relive its mistakes.

—from *The Messenger*, April 24, 1985, Simpson United Methodist Church, Pullman, Washington.

We live in a world obsessed with violence, war and death. Here, for the anniversary of Iraq War II, I present a hymn written at the beginning of Iraq War I . . . The Gulf War.

The Palouse Papers

A Hymn for Lent in a Time of War—March 1991

Tunes: LM 88.88 such as: Hursley LM #468 United Methodist Hymnal—Maryton #430 UMH—Hamburg #298 UMH Deus Tuorum Militum LM #634 United Methodist Hymnal—#83 Lutheran Book of Worship

1. O God, the pure in heart are blessed,
But what of us, whose deeds confess
Our hearts are hard, and cold as stone?
Can you for us our sin atone?

2. We should for you renounce our pride,
For Christ who for our sins has died,
Yet we afraid to share his pain,
Would lose our souls, the world to gain.

3. Our power blinds our eyes to see
The neighbor in our enemy,
The friend that hides within the foe,
The child of God we fail to know.

4. Not force of arms but love alone
Can heal our hearts, our sin atone,
Will wound our pride, and let us be
At last at peace, where all are free.

5. O Christ, who meets our deepest need,
Who for our pain and guilt did bleed,
Grant us by grace, the power to see
Your vision of the world to be.

6. Let every nation, every tongue,
Confess that all to you belong,
Enable us at last to know
Your love for all, that peace may grow.

—from *The Messenger*, Simpson United Methodist Church, Pullman,
Washington, March 1991, *Hymns for All Seasons*, 1992.

The Port Angeles Papers

Is God Gay? . . . or Straight? . . . Both? Or Neither?

Recent news items have brought to public attention the discussion and conflict within the United Methodist Church over the various issues surrounding the topic of homosexuality. This discussion has been taking place in our denomination and several others for many years now. It has produced a lot of conflict and tension as well as fruitful exchange of ideas for a long time. It has also diverted us from other tasks that are equally if not far more important.

Our Bishop, Elias Galvan, along with other bishops of our church, has requested we have discussions of these issues in our congregations as the Conference seeks to discern what God's will might be in such matters. So, for the record, here is whatever contribution I, as your Pastor, would make regarding this vast and complex subject of homosexuals in the church.

First, let me say that nearly every congregation I have served has included persons of homosexual orientation within its fellowship. Sometimes these persons were "in the closet" [often for the sake of their families] and could relate their anguish, need and questions regarding their situation only to the Pastor or a few other members they could confide in. Others were known to be of this orientation and were accepted and loved by the other church members without reservation. I have never served a congregation that excluded people because of their sexual orientation.

The current discussion around the issue of homosexuality in the church is complicated by the introduction of "sexual politics," involving organized efforts to seek to force the issue on the church and demand inclusion or exclusion of people on all sides of these questions. Two forms that this has taken in the debate are the following movements in our denomination and others:

On the one side there is an effort to establish "Reconciling Congregations," i.e., those who overtly declare themselves to be congregations that openly and deliberately accept homosexual persons into their fellowship as a matter of church policy and public action, and thereby announce to the world that they are without discrimination in these matters.

On the other side of the argument there is now a movement to establish what has been termed "Transforming Congregations," i.e., those who declare themselves congregations that believe homosexual persons can be changed through repentance, prayer and counseling, and that the "recovery rate" for such persons is better than that for alcoholics.

Both of these movements in the church can cite clinical evidence, scriptural witness, and "theological" justification for their activities, contentions against each other, and I might say, against the church at large.

Frankly, I am weary of such nonsense. And, if I may speak even more candidly here, I need to assert that both of these movements are theologically naive, biblically illiterate, intellectually simplistic, politically arrogant and ecclesiastically dangerous.

Do "Reconciling Congregations" really mean to infer that those who don't wear this label are not into reconciliation? Do "Transforming Congregations" really mean to imply that those who do not wear *this* label do not believe in transformation? What arrogance! What a put down to all who won't sign up!

Should we have a "reconciling congregation" on one corner, and a "transforming congregation" on the other? Should we form new "Conferences" . . . each consisting of different kinds of "congregations?" How sad this has all become!

It seems to me that any Christian, even a few yards beyond baptism, ought to be able to see through political chicanery such as this. Since when does acceptance of one another imply *endorsement* of all of each other's views or style, agendas or convictions? We are not into bumper sticker discipleship. We are into breadth and depth. Or are we?

Any congregation that is the Church of Jesus Christ is into reconciliation and transformation at the same time and all the time or it is not the church of Jesus Christ. Both are essential to being the Church of Jesus

Christ. You can't be for reconciliation and not for transformation! Reconciliation implies transformation! Transformation implies reconciliation! And in far more ways than simply around the issues of sexuality. All are welcome into this fellowship . . . where "we shall all be changed!"

Any congregation can and should have ministries with a special focus, intention and support, as we do here. But to *define the congregation* as oriented toward a single issue or area of concern is to reduce the being and nature of the church to but a shadow of what it is called to be. This is ecclesiastical reductionism of a very simplistic sort.

So just what is going on here?

What is going on is that we are witnessing the exploitation of great biblical words and magnificent theological understandings of the Gospel of Christ by single-issue politics on both sides of these questions. And what is going on is that this exploitation on behalf of this "single-issue politics" threatens to destroy the church.

God sent Christ into the world; *this* world full of all kinds of people: straight and gay, male and female, truthful and dishonest, caring and indifferent, sinful and repentant, and whatever . . . to show us how to love one another, accept one another, and be transformed and reconciled beyond our wildest dreams, by the grace shown to us in that same Christ!

In God's name and for God's sake . . . Let us "let the Church be the Church," not just some political action committee. Let us be the church of Christ where "whoever will may come"—where whoever is called may serve, and where all are the recipients of the incredible grace and mercy of God!

May Grace, which is Transformation, and Peace, which is Reconciliation, be to you and to all of us!

—from "A View from the Tower," *The Tower Echoes*, 1998, Port Angeles United Methodist and Congregational Church, Port Angeles, Washington.

A Good Laugh for Lent

One of the greatest witnesses to the power and reality of God I ever experienced was in a short utterance by Frank Goodnough, the Director of the Wesley Foundation at the University of Washington, when I was a student. I was reading a book on the life of John Wesley in preparation for getting my "Preacher's License." I was really impressed with what I read about the great founder of the Methodist movement. I shared my admiration for John Wesley with "Mr. G." He listened attentively, let out one of the heartiest laughs I have ever heard and then exclaimed . . . "John Wesley! *He* was just an office boy!"

Somehow, that was worth several semesters of systematic theology!

We are nearing the end of the Lenten season—following Jesus to Jerusalem and the Cross. It is in this season that we discover who he *really* is. We witness this awesome love of God that both enabled and compelled Jesus to go wide-eyed into certain disaster. For us! We sing hymns like "What wondrous love is this?" . . . Or, "Jesus, Keep Me Near the Cross . . ." We try to get more serious about our faith, and consider disciplines to help us do so.

We used to talk about giving something up for Lent. We are all too aware that we are more likely to give up Lent for something else. We discover that like the rest of humankind—we "cannot bear too much reality." We would rather have a sort of "cheerleader" Christ than this "Man of Sorrows." We discover that we, like the first disciples, are not up to such heroic obedience to the demands of love. We too would run away and hide, deny we knew him, desert him, and even betray him with a kiss. Indeed, such love "turns followers into fools, and fractures all our bones of pride." We aren't even "office boys" in this firm of divine management. Like his first disciples, we find other things to do. He goes to his cross at last . . . alone.

So why the hearty laugh? If James and John, and Saul of Tarsus, and Priscilla and Aquila, and Catherine of Siena, and Luther and Calvin and John Wesley were only lowly office help, then what hope is there for us?

It is here we discover that Lent is the preparation for Easter . . . not

Good Friday. We can't handle Good Friday. But Easter! . . . Easter takes hold . . . of us! Easter turns failed disciples into blazing Apostles! Damned fools into "fools for Christ!" Saul into Paul! Broken priests like John Wesley into grateful "office boys!" A tiny nun from the most backward country in Europe into Mother Theresa of Calcutta who would rather comfort the dying than get the Nobel Prize! That is why these sort of people write about "Amazing Grace" and long for "a thousand tongues to sing!" Or, they say with David Livingston, "I never made a sacrifice in my life," supremely aware of the one made for them. They, who discovered themselves unworthy to tie his sandals, would shine shoes for this Christ, who took a towel and washed their feet!

Watch out world! Here they come! Nothing can stop them now! "How beautiful upon the mountains" they are—bringing good tidings!

We now look at Lent as a time to give to others rather than give up something for a few weeks . . . perhaps feeding our pride. Maybe we need to develop a hearty "Lenten laugh" . . . knowing that we who wanted to be the Boss will by his grace be more than happy to serve where we can!

That's why I heard the hearty laugh! "John Wesley! *He* was just an office boy!" . . . For behind the man is . . . "Behold! THE MAN" . . . the One . . . who is . . . the LORD!

A hearty Lenten laugh! And a joyous Easter to you!—His servants!

Your Pastor . . . just another helper in the "office."

The Palouse Papers

A Parable of Lights

The pastor was in a hurry. It was Holy Week and the beginning of the Great Three Days of the Christian Passover. His people were gathering for a soup and bread supper, followed by the Holy Thursday Communion and the Service of Shadows.

Suddenly one of his parishioners stopped him in the hallway and told him that there was someone who wished to speak with him. He turned and was introduced to a student from the university who said that she was enrolled in a class where she had an assignment to video-tape a commercial, and that she would like permission to bring a crew of students to film it in our church parking lot.

"When?" said the pastor, probably too abruptly, but catching himself in the awareness that she was a foreign student.

"How about Friday night?" she said.

"Friday?" he replied, "but that's *G o o d   F r i d a y* and it's not really" he paused, noticing that this got no reaction of recognition from her at all.

"How about Saturday night?" she said.

"That's not a good time either, as we are having a service here . . . the *Great Vigil of Easter* . . . you see, this is *E a s t e r*," he began to explain . . . still noticing no recognition of what that might mean.

"Sunday night?" she said.

He paused again, in the realization that the life and activities of the church were something that were just not a part of her experience. He lost his sense of hurry and annoyance for a moment and asked her where she was from and what she was studying, and how she liked living here. They then agreed that she would call him to firm up a time when she could tape the commercial.

As she began to leave he couldn't help but ask, "Would you mind telling me why you want to film a TV commercial in our church parking lot?"

"Oh," she said, "you have such wonderful lights!"

"Lights?" he said.

"Yes, your church has such powerful lights on your parking lot. It's an ideal place to shoot a television commercial."

"Yes," he replied . . . "we do have some very good lights on our parking lot."

They said goodbye, and parted . . . and he went in to the *Holy Thursday* supper, and she went out . . . "and it was night."

Somehow his heart was heavy . . . and then suddenly he said to himself, "*Why didn't you invite her to have supper with us! You fool! What kind of a 'light' are you . . .?*"

Then he quickly realized that this stranger who came to him by night had just engaged him in a kind of living parable. His annoyance at being interrupted in his haste, and his despair at what seemed to be an encroaching darkness, somehow turned into a kind of gratitude for what now seemed a strange but grace-filled intrusion.

Two nights later, on *Easter Eve*, in the *Vigil* service, after dozens of candles were glowing in the dark nave of the church, he shared this "parable" with his people, observing how he was increasingly aware that the Church must come to the realization that we are a minority people in the world . . . a world that has neither heard nor responded to the Gospel. The "lights" of the church that seem to impress this world are on our parking lots . . . not on our faces. And on this *Eve of Easter* . . . this "night of nights" . . . when we have said:

May the light of Christ, rising in glory,
banish the darkness of our hearts and minds,

We need to rediscover our calling to share a different kind of light with the world than the floodlights on our parking lot, or the dozens of candles in a beautiful service.

We are called to share the "light of Christ" . . . the Light of the World—who says again to his people, "*you* are the light of the world. Let your light so shine that the world may see your good works and give glory to your Father who is in heaven."

May that light of Christ . . . rising in glory . . . banish the darkness of *our* hearts and minds, that we might become again . . . in his name . . . "the light of the world." A glorious Eastertide to you!

—from *The Messenger,* Simpson United Methodist Church, March 30, 1989,
Pullman, Washington.

To Be and Not to Be . . . and Yet to Be Again

To be or not to be—that is the question

—Shakespeare: Hamlet III. i.

We should have guessed it
From the gentle hint of the
Pale signature[1] at the flash point
Of the becoming world—
Turning our faces toward
The growing dawn.

We should have guessed
That the end of all this way
Was already there as a new beginning,[2]
And that to be, and not to be,
And yet to be again,
Is really the un-acknowledged answer
Of the question[3] we were only too
Content to merely ask.

When the world was young and
Easy[4] under the blessing burdened boughs,
About to break with glory
On our very heads;
We turned away,
And shut our ears to the
Gentle summons in the gracious evening,[5]
That would breathe to birth
A bright new world within our hearts.

Instead, fearful and lonely[6]
Amid the shadows of the day,
We named our dying light
A candle brief[7] against the impending dark,
And saw ourselves the broken actors
In a play that failed
On a broad way that led
To our demise.[8]

We did not go gently,
But raved and raged[9] until
The time for the offering of the oblation[10]
On that dark and Friday noon,[11]
When the burning Love who brought
To birth the dawn of life
Was stilled, and turned into the shining
Axis of the twirling world.[12]

Awakened from our sleep
Of death,[13] we found ourselves
Surprised at last[14] to have our question
Answered by the Master light
Of all our seeing—[15]
With new and radiant eyes
We gazed in wonder on
The Glory
Of our honored kind—[16]

Who was, was not, and yet
Forever is—again.[17]

—from A Word in Season, Graham Hutchins.

NOTES

1. Dylan Thomas: "In the beginning was the pale signature, . . ." from *In the beginning . . .*

2. T. S. Eliot: ". . . The end is where we start from" from *Little Gidding*, cf. also *East Coker in Four Quartets*.
3. William Shakespeare: "To be or not to be—that is the question: *Hamlet*: III.i
4. Dylan Thomas: "When I was young and easy under the apple boughs . . ." from *Fern Hill*
5. Genesis 3:8-9
6. W.H. Auden: cf. September 1, 1939, or, "Alone, alone about a dreadful wood of conscious evil runs a lost mankind . . ."
7. William Shakespeare: *Macbeth* V.v.
8. Matthew. 7:13
9. Dylan Thomas: "Do not go gentle into that good night, . . . Rage, rage, against the dying of the light." 1 Kings 18:20-29.
10. 1 Kings 18:36
11. G. Hutchins: from: "Some Seasoned Words," in *Some Words for All Seasons*
12. T. S. Eliot: "Against the Word the unstilled world still whirled, About the centre of the silent Word." from *Ash Wednesday* V
13. Isaiah 60:1-3; Ephesians 45:14-15; Romans 13:11-12
14. Gerard Manley Hopkins: "In a flash, at a trumpet crash, I am all at once what Christ is since he was what I am, . . ." from *That Nature is a Heraclitean Fire and the Comfort of the Resurrection*
15. William Wordsworth: from *Intimations of Immortality Seen in Early Childhood*
16. Psalms 8, Hebrews 2:9
17. Revelation 1:18.

The Palouse Papers

Spring Comes to the Channeled Scablands

It being essential
To traverse this nowhere
Between destinations,
One can ignore the barren landscape
Where ancient floods scoured these
Massive forms into this
Wasteland of the mind.

And yet, in early Spring,
While traveling alone,
I saw that even here,
On a long drive east toward home,
How because of gentle rain
On the dry and desolate stone,
There could now be seen amidst the
Brittle dead and wasted grass—
New life—the subtle sheen of green.

In the desolation of these days—
And the folly of our ways
Are we moved to offer praise
To the One who through our pain
Grants us love like gentle rain?
Can our hearts begin to sing of
The fresh new signs of Spring?

As you journey toward your home,
Are you traveling alone?
Does this parable of Spring
And the sheen of gentle green
Speak a word you need to hear,
That new life may now appear?
Among the brittle wasted grass
Of the growth that is our past,
Could we ask our God to bring
The subtle sheen of Spring?

In the scablands of the heart
Let the gentle graces start,
Through basaltic plates of pride,
Channel contours that abide,
In the dry fall of our years
Grow the garden of your tears.
On this arid world and mean,
Bring the sudden sheen of green.

Note: The Channeled Scablands are the result of massive floods at the end of the Ice Age that carved channels through the basaltic lava flow layers of the Columbia Plateau in central Washington. The river changed its course to the west on what is now called the Big Bend of the Columbia leaving the old riverbed virtually bereft of water except for a few mostly arid lakes. The Channeled Scablands are a series of gashes in the land that extend from near Coulee City southward over what is now called Dry Falls to connect with the present Snake and Columbia river basins to the south and west.

The Port Angeles Papers

Cape Disappointment?

The trail wound steeply down through the forest and then ascended the opposite ridge to the oldest lighthouse in the Northwest. It stands high above the mouth of the Columbia River, where early explorers by sea thought they had found the western entrance of the fabled Northwest Passage—a passage to India like a canal, through the immense American land mass, linking Europe and the exotic East. This is also the place where Lewis and Clark first saw the Pacific, that great western sea toward which they had been toiling for months on end over a vast wilderness of prairies, rivers and mountains. Here, where one of the great rivers of the continent meets the awesome Pacific, so much longing, wonder, adventure, exploration and history converge. Here—certainly—should be a notable lighthouse as well as a place of celebration. You'd think the promontory would be called something like *Cape Achievement* or *Cape Discovery*—like the *Cape of Good Hope* at the southern tip of Africa.

Yet this awesome sight bears a curious name . . . *Cape Disappointment*. Captain John Meares, no mean sailor, called it such because he couldn't get over the sand bar at the river's mouth from the sea. Frustrated and feeling defeated in his efforts he projected his despair onto the nearby headland and gave it a most unfortunate and unlikely name for the meeting place of great adventures of exploration and discovery like his own and later those of Lewis and Clark. It is an impressive place and we wondered at the incongruity of its designation.

Could it be that those involved in great causes are so often concerned with the task at hand or some other narrow focus of their vision that they are hardly aware of where they are? One can be in a very significant place or in relationship to some awfully important stuff and be terribly disappointed because it doesn't meet your narrowly defined purpose or expectation.

Peggy Lee used to sing a song that ranged through many of the experiences of life. In response to everything from a circus, to a fire, to romance, to marriage, to life itself . . . was a sad and constant refrain: "Is that all there is?" The song asserts that "all there is" in this life is disappointment. Disappointment had become a god. Everything was summed up in being let down.

Jacob had a dream while running away from his angry brother Esau. He was filled with fear and guilt and loneliness when he slept with a stone for a pillow in a dark and forbidding place. Yet he awoke in astonished awareness that the Lord was in that place, and that it was "none other than the house of God and the gate of heaven!"

A vast and magnificent place called *Cape Disappointment*. A desolate place that becomes the awesome *House of God*.

How about the church?

I am continually astonished as a Pastor to realize that the same place, the same events, and the same people can become for some "none other than the house of God and the gate of heaven" and to others a kind of *Cape Disappointment*. How about you?

We live in a consumer culture. We like to evaluate churches as we do shopping malls. It all depends on what you can *get* there. If we don't find it we may say, "Is that all there is?" Maybe we have forgotten something . . . that "it is in *giving* we receive." We might discover we have "all this and heaven too!"

The church can be a source of frustration and disappointment to us because we don't find what we want, or we can't get our way; or it can be where we find a new life and are "surprised by joy!" Look around . . . dream some dreams . . . seek reconciliation . . . open your heart and mind. Let God have his way with you!

Can any place or land or church become a "land of promise"?

Maybe your own *Cape Disappointment* can turn into a place of glorious vistas, exploration, and discovery!

—View from the Tower—*The Tower Echoes*, 1996.

The Palouse Papers

To Be Free or Not to Be, That Is the Question

"Democracy is the worst form of government in the world, except for all those other systems."

—Winston Churchill

"Because of the good in man democracy is possible, because of the evil in man, democracy is necessary."

—Reinhold Niebuhr

". . . seek the welfare of the city to which I have sent you into exile, and pray to the LORD on its behalf, for in its welfare you will find your welfare."

—Jeremiah 29:7

There is a profound restlessness in our land. There is also a profound frustration in the gathering momentum as our nation prepares to elect new leadership to the highest offices of government in the country. In frustration, many people are not going to vote at all. In desperation, many will vote for what they perceive to be the lesser of two evils. With enthusiasm, some are going to vote for what they consider is a bright hope for our future. In indifference, many will care less and let others shape their destiny.

A little over a year ago, while in Chile, we attended a Bible study at a little congregation in a poor section of Santiago, served by one of our United Methodist missionaries. The theme of the study they began that night was a biblical look at *The Christian and Civic Responsibility*. The leaders of the church were hoping to enable their people to get enough

27

courage to vote their convictions in the election that was coming some fourteen months later. There would be no choice of candidates on the ballot. The only name that would appear was that of the dictator, Augusto Pinochet. The only choice they would have would be to vote *Yes* or *No*. They would need courage to vote *No*. This South American country with the greatest tradition of democratic government on the continent was now a police state. To vote *No*, or in any way be critical of the government, meant one could suddenly disappear and never be heard from again. Or, it might mean the loss of employment, or torture or death. The Chilean people needed courage and hope. They were in exile in their own land. To seek the good of their country took courage. Courage to vote *against* the government. Courage to vote *NO!*

Last month they voted. And they voted their convictions over-whelmingly—they voted *N O !* And the next day the streets were filled with hundreds of thousands of people celebrating the fact that they had summoned the courage to vote and thereby to say *NO!* to tyranny and brutal police power, which had stifled freedom in their land. It was an awesome sight. They sought the good of the country in which they felt like exiles, even though it was their own. They knew that in its welfare would be their own. They cared enough to dare enough to vote their convictions and repudiate a dictator.

This year we vote. Or will we? It is a startling fact that of all the de-mocracies in the world, ours is the one with the lowest participation at the ballot box. We—who pride ourselves on our freedom. We—who think we live in the greatest nation in the world. We—who have the right to vote or not to vote, but who thereby have the right and the privi-lege and the duty to vote . We—who can vote without fear of recrimina-tion, without fear of the police, or torture, or death. It doesn't take a lot of courage to vote here. You don't lay your life on the line to show up at the polling place to cast your ballot. But we still should seek the good of the country where we live. Many of us are beginning to feel like exiles in an increasingly strange land. Many of us think we have never had it so good. Both groups might be right. For some, it is "Morning in America." For others, it is approaching midnight. All should be concerned to seek the good of the country where they live. In its prosperity and welfare is their welfare and prosperity. It may not take courage to vote in America today. It should take commitment. Some day—if we lack conviction and concern—it might take courage. Chile was a democracy. It had to desperately seek to become one again. What about us? We are a democracy. Will we remain one?

It has been well said, "Eternal vigilance is the price of liberty." Let us seek the good of the country where we are . . . at home or in exile at home . . . and pray to the LORD on its behalf, for in its welfare is our own.

—from The Messenger, Simpson United Methodist Church, Pullman,
Washington, 1988.

The Port Angeles Papers

What If the Ships No Longer Came this Way . . .

What if the ships no longer came this way,
and we were left here
upon this lonely coast,
To wonder why the world broke down.

What if no trees were left to fall
and all the logs were gone,
The great trucks reduced to hauling sticks,
And loggers only found in country songs?

Suppose no fish were left to spawn
As rivers spill their silt from clear-cut hills
where no birds nest or sing,
On stumps like gravestones aging in the sun.

Imagine all the mills shut down,
And we could breathe clean air in unemployment lines,
Surrender hope to the prevailing winds,
and huddle with the homeless poor.

Do you really think we could make a living
hunting and gathering on the gaming wheels of chance,
Hoping to harpoon the city slickers
lured to come their way?

If we turned this place into
a barren waste . . .
Would the light still fall upon these rooms
as the seasons spin,
To amaze us into wonder with a
sudden burst of glory?
That compass-rose on an ancient map
summoned into blazing by the winter sun,
Just burned into my mind from off
the study wall;
A shooting star destined for a
dazzling moment.

Look! There comes a ship!
From what distant, exotic ports of call
over the vast oceans
Does it sail into this Strait and
narrow way?
Perhaps it brings unusual merchandise
to trade for logs or fish or grain?
Its crew to gaze upon our mountains
and wonder what enticing cities
line these shores?

My friends . . .
The hour lies late upon the world . . .
But great ships come with cargoes yet,
the birds still sing,
some salmon spawn,
a forest teems with life,
And we can glimpse the dancing of
the evening light
across the study wall.

What gifts of wonder!
Will the night remove?
Or shall we see bright lights upon
the other shore,
And wait new dawn to aid our watch
for ships
That sail into our lives
and bring romantic worlds
to call?

—from *A Word in Season*, 1998.

The Palouse Papers

True Freedom

The season of Lent is a time every year of profound reflection on our spiritual condition. Or should we say—Lent used to be? It was a time when we confronted some uncomfortable truths about ourselves and sought to amend our lives in the light of God's saving acts on our behalf. Lent was a centering exercise in which we discovered ourselves as our own worst enemies, and sought to go in a new direction. This was called repentance. It was a time when, like the Prodigal Son, we "came to ourselves" and started for home.

The other day on the radio I heard an amazing statement. Someone was commenting on the London bookmakers' odds on our presidential candidates, and observed in passing that:

"Those who tell the truth are gone. Are out of the race. Are finished as candidates. Haven't got a chance for the nomination, much less win the election. Are a poor bet indeed."

This, it seems to me, is more than a passing comment. It is an awesome comment . A very significant comment. Talk about a *Thought for the Day!* This is a "thought for the year!" Because, if it is true—we as a nation are in deep trouble.

I believe it is a true statement. And its impact lies not in the fact that it is a commentary on the candidates, but on *us* . . . the people . . . and on the ways we have devised to elect our leadership. If the candidates for the highest office in our land cannot tell us the truth without losing all chance at the nomination—then we are in trouble indeed—and deserve the bad government we elect.

Could it be that we have slept through a profound change in our body politic? Like some Rip Van Winkle . . . do we wake to a new order of reality and not even understand that this isn't the nation we knew? If we will elect only those who will not tell us the truth, then we have already succumbed to the *Big Lie.* If a people cannot deal with the truth about their world, then they are either mentally ill or on their way there. If the real truth about what we have become is so devastating that knowledge of it would rip the nation apart—then all our defenses won't defend us, all our spending won't save us, all our posturing about our great nation is hot air. If all our pious rhetoric is blasphemy, then all our boasting is shown up for the vanity that it really is—the pride that goes before the fall.

"You shall know the truth," said Jesus, "and the truth shall make you free." What happens when a people who pride themselves on being free, are afraid to hear the truth? And who would refuse to elect to high office anyone who dared to tell them the truth? The truth about such a people is that they are no longer free—but slaves to untruth—that is, the victim of lies. Such a people need no enemy to conquer them, they have defeated themselves. They are headed for a fall—as the Roman Empire fell—even if they conquer the world.

Have we already met our biggest and most dangerous enemy—and found it is us? We may like to think we live safely in "Fortress America"—but, like the Prodigal, we might really be in the "far country" . . . far from our true home and our native land. Perhaps as a people, not just as individuals, it's time to face some truth about ourselves, painful as it is—and head for home. Can a nation repent, and go in a new direction? Maybe these things are worth thinking about all this year. We might just come to know and understand some things that are truly helpful. Then, maybe the truth will set us free.

—Thought for the Day, *The Pullman Herald*, February 24, 1988.

The Palouse Papers

Some Notes for a Prayer at the Commencement

Washington State University, May 7, 1988

O God, in whom we live and move and have our being:
We thank you for this day . . .
    In which we may remember . . .
    On which we can celebrate . . .
    From which we can hope . . .

In the presence of our families, our friends, our teachers,
    our students,
Our leaders in this university,
    And those who provide for us and represent us in high office in
    our land . . .

Help us this day to remember . . .
    The patience it takes to truly learn;
    The learning it takes to really know;
    The knowing it takes to finally understand;
    The understanding it takes to genuinely care;
    The caring it takes to truly teach;
    The teaching it takes to fully love;
    And the loving it takes to finally *be*.
O God . . . Help us to remember . . .

Help us this day to celebrate . . .
    The joy of beginnings . . .
    The pride of achievement . . . the lessons of failure . . .
    The rigors of discipline . . . the peace of conclusion . . .
    The excitement of discovery . . .
    The satisfactions of sharing . . .
    The beauty of insight . . . and the possibility of wisdom.
O God . . . help us to celebrate . . .

Help us this day to hope . . .
    That our careers may become a calling . . .
    That our rewards may be more than our earnings . . .
    That our skills be useful in the service of others.
    That our knowledge may do some good . . .
    That our lives may be glad that we were here . . .
    And that our world may be a better place because
    we were . . .
O God . . . help us to hope . . .

O God . . .
    Whose being is Love . . .
    Whose love can teach us to care . . . to understand . . .
    and to know . . .
Grant us the patience we need to truly learn . . .
    For in your truth is our wisdom . . .
    In your will is our peace . . .
    And in your love is our hope . . .

Bless us . . . each . . . and all . . . this day . . .
    we pray . . . AMEN

The Palouse Papers

A Hymn for Easter

Tune: Grafton 87.87.87. #505 United Methodist Hymnal—Tantum Ergo Sacramentum #207 The Church Hymnary

1. Christ has broken all the chains that bound him!
Christ has triumphed o're the grave!
Christ is risen! Let us all adore him!
Risen! All the earth to save!
Alleluia! Alleluia!
Alleluia! Christ is risen from the grave!

2. Death itself, it could not hold him!
Christ our Lord, the Crucified!
He has conquered! Now behold him!
Raised from death and glorified!
Alleluia! Alleluia!
Lives again the One who for our sins had died!

3. We ourselves are risen with him!
Risen to new life again!
We at last will live before him,
Singing out the glad refrain!
Alleluia! Alleluia!
Alleluia! Let the great Amen begin.

4. Now all nations will confess him!
All on earth their glad shout raise!
Let all peoples come before him,
Singing our Redeemer's praise!
Alleluia! Alleluia!
Alleluia! Alleluia! and Amen!

—from Hymns for All Seasons, 1990.

The Port Angeles Papers

The Bright Cloud—Transfiguration on Ediz Hook

One Sunday afternoon last fall we took a drive out to Ediz Hook, that marvelous spit of land that reaches out into the Strait of Juan de Fuca and thereby forms the harbor of Port Angeles. After a busy preacher's Sunday morning, a good dinner and a brief read of the newspaper we decided to take a short nap, right there in our car by the boat landing.

We woke up a few minutes later to one of the amazing natural phenomena of this area. The sun was shining . . . but we were in the fog! A bright cloud was all about us . . . and the warmth of the sun covered us with a gentle glow and yet we could no longer see the city and the mountains, nor even the harbor or the shore, but only the radiant glory of the cloud.

Now those who have lived here for some time might take all of this for granted, but if you haven't been living near the sea, or done a lot of flying or mountain climbing lately, this is a rare sight.

Then, suddenly the voice of the nearby foghorn came out of the cloud with what almost seemed to us to be a shout of *Glory!* This was vivid data for a marvelous sort of parable, this experience of sudden awareness that is almost biblical in its impact. To the Hebrew mind, such experiences pointed beyond themselves to an encounter with the

God of creation and became the means whereby God was revealed in startling and mysterious ways.

What is there about such an experience that astonishes one into a sense of wonder? For most people, a cloud is that which brings darkness upon the land. We have all observed the sun shining on great clouds in the distance, but when the clouds are overhead or one is within them one usually experiences a sense of darkness or even gloom, and wishes the clouds would drift away and the sun would shine again.

Whence then comes this sun filled cloud? Is it sort of like the bush that burned and was not consumed that Moses saw in the wilderness of Sinai? This sight too, was a cause for amazement and for wonder at this sudden surprise . . . *a bright cloud.*

The image brings to mind another biblical event. It was on that long ago day when the disciples were summoned by Jesus to go up onto a mountain . . . apart from the teeming throngs of people . . . from all that need and demand and confusion . . . and there *"he was transfigured before them, and his face shown like the sun, and his garments became white as light . . . and there appeared to them Moses and Elijah, talking with him."* Peter . . . amazed . . . stammered something about how good it was to be there . . . and then we read, *"and a* bright cloud *overshadowed them, and a voice from the cloud said, 'This is my beloved Son, with whom I am well pleased; listen to him' and when the disciples heard this, they fell on their faces, and were filled with awe."*

This cloud, this voice, this encounter that filled them with such awe, indicates that they are in the very presence of the very God . . . who is Light of light and God of gods. Paradox alone can describe such an experience. How does such a bright cloud . . . "overshadow" one? Shadows are the absence of light . . . this was the presence of light. Clouds cast a shadow. This cloud radiated glory. This is a way of speaking about God that indicates both God's hidden-ness and God's revelation. God, as it were, hides in a bright cloud, so we won't be blinded by light . . . but at the same time experience God's glory. So too, in our own encounters with the holy, that which "overshadows" us is the glory of God . . . and we are filled with awe.

We were not with Jesus on the holy mountain of Transfiguration long ago, but my wife and I had something of a sense of what it might have been like . . . one Sunday afternoon out at Ediz Hook, when we should have felt lost in the fog, but were instead surrounded with a radiant cloud of glory, and we are grateful.

—from Transfiguration, 1994 and "A View from the Tower," *The Tower Echoes*, First United Methodist and Congregational Church, Port Angeles, Washington.

The Port Angeles Papers

The Dark Tower

While returning across the strait from Victoria one evening last fall we witnessed one of the most dazzling sunsets I have ever experienced. The whole sky was afire with glory. Most of the passengers on the MV *Coho* watched the spectacle with a sense of awe. Cameras couldn't begin to do it justice. We scanned the sky and the horizon transfigured by the wonder of it all.

Suddenly I noticed what appeared to be the shadow of a ship or and island off to the west and barely visible on the radiant line between sea and sky. We reached for the binoculars and after a few minutes discerned that it was the dark shadow of a tower of some sort silhouetted against the blazing glory of the evening. What could it be?

Several more minutes passed and we discerned that it was indeed a tower . . . the dark tower of a lighthouse! I found myself gazing at this strange sight . . . the *shadow* of a lighthouse! Against the backdrop of the flaming sky we could barely distinguish the methodical flashing of the light atop this dark tower, almost as if it was rehearsing offstage for the coming drama of the night. What a tiny light against the fiery sun! What an anomaly! The first thing we saw in that glowing seascape was the dark shadow of a lighthouse!

Scarcely an hour later the only thing we could see was the light and not the tower. By then the sun was gone from our view and the lighthouse was a beacon piercing the vast darkness of the world.

Here is a kind of parable . . . almost the opposite of *The Bright Cloud* of earlier reflection in this column. As that was an image of the glory of God . . . hidden, yet revealed, this one seems to me to be a parable of the relation of the light to the Light. The light of the church and our witness to the glory of God we see in the face of the Son.

To many, the church and its message is a kind of *dark tower* on the horizon of their lives. Scarcely noticed . . . easily ignored . . . hardly relevant to their own purposes, work, families, etc. Their daily routine has no need of such distractions. In their busy lives even the Sun is taken for granted, so why bother with the Son?

But let the darkness descend, and the night come upon them and their usual ways lead suddenly to nowhere—they often find how desperately they need a light to find their way again. It is then that they discover that the little light this strange dark tower provides can even save their lives, and that it points beyond itself to the "very hidden source of all our seeing" that is the Light of light . . . which is God.

We dare not look into the face of the Sun—even the light of a lighthouse could blind us—these are what we see *by*, not something we can see. But those, who on the journey of their lives have been privileged to see, as St. Paul observed, "the light of the knowledge of the glory of God" reflected in the face of Christ—those who are his Church—discover that they—even they—are the custodians and stewards of his light and vision.

We, who in this place and time are privileged to be his Church, are the keepers of his lighthouse upon the dark seas of human history. We need to let the light he gives us shine, so people can find their way, "until the Daystar rises in their hearts" . . . and then, together with us they will "give glory to the God of heaven."

—from "A View from the Tower," *The Tower Echoes*, Summer 1994, First United Methodist and Congregational Church, Port Angeles, Washington.

Everywhere

In the Name of One Who Nails the World Down . . .

Unless somewhere
    becomes wherever,
    anywhere is nowhere,
     and forever.
All maps run out,
    and journeys end
     in silence.
The race is neither to the swift or slow,
     and shouldn't have been run at all.
Then every gain is finally loss,
     and sums are minus,
Each place is really no place,
     our meeting only parting,
Love's labor's lost at last,
     and so are lovers,
For nowhere then is everywhere
     and nothing.

But should
    somewhere become
Wherever two or three are gathered
     in the name of One who nails
      the world down in its place;
     then everywhere is somewhere,
     and forever!
Our journeys end in joy!
     And all roads lead to home,
The lost is found, and turns
     to gain, and not in vain

        our labor then, when
Everywhere is somewhere
        wherever Love is
        known.

—from All Words for Some Seasons, 1992.

The Palouse Papers

License Plate Theology

Summer is coming! For many that means traveling, if only for a weekend or two. After a long winter we like to hit the road and get a change of scenery and find some relaxation.

For some this means long trips with the kids in the car and playing a game where we try to identify as many different license plates as possible. We've also said goodbye to lots of friends this spring that then loaded up their cars and drove off into the future elsewhere. Some of them will be located in places where they will have to get new license plates.

I read an observation by Frederick Buechner to the effect that license plates on our automobiles are witnesses both to the presence of Christ and the indifference of humanity. We don't often think of such things when we think of license plates. Usually we are mindful of how expensive they can be in Washington and how cheap they are in Oregon! Or we may think of someone we know or someplace we've been when we see a plate from another state or province.

So what is the theology of license plates? How do they bear witness to Christ? Think about it. Every car has a plate with a renewal date on it. I just got some that say, Mar 90—this to remind me that I must renew that license in March of the year of our Lord 1990. There it is! Every such plate reminds us of the date of Christ's birth.

Think of all the people driving around swearing at other drivers in

41

the name of Christ and totally oblivious of the fact that their vehicle bears witness to the birth of Christ! But this means that license plates are also a witness to human indifference.

Maybe it's like bread. Bread is just bread. Common daily sustenance. We're glad it's there, but so what? Yet for those who have shared in the bread of the Lord's table and begin to realize what it means, bread is not *just* bread anymore. Whenever they see bread they are reminded of One who took bread, blessed it, broke it, and gave it, and said, "This is my body" . . . Bread can't be merely bread anymore. It speaks of Christ. So may it be with other things—like license plates.

Wherever you drive this summer—even if only to the grocery store to get some bread—take note—along the highway, in the parking lots, or on a quiet street—everywhere you go in this world that seems so indifferent to Christ—you will see witnesses of Christ! Signs of renewal on the license plates of the indifferent world! Signs of one who came to "renew" the world—who paid the price for *our* renewal, and by whose gracious permission we are free to travel on! Good traveling to you!

—from *The Messenger*, Simpson United Methodist Church, Pullman, Washington, May 25, 1989.

Hutchaeme, Port Angeles, July 3, 2004

Some Cautionary Tales . . . But We Are Still Here!

As we as a nation celebrate and observe our Independence Day on the 4th of July, it is a time not just for fireworks and picnics, but of memory and hope. This 228th anniversary of our nation is cause for grateful reflection on that which we have achieved but also a time of concern for what we are again in danger of losing, and perhaps an occasion for sharing hopes of a renewal of our national life in this great republic.

To that end, this edition of *Paper Trails* invites you to look over my shoulder with me to previous moments of memory and hope in other contexts. They come from several sources and are color-coded and/or in different fonts to help you find your way! So reminisce with me in thoughts from 1999, 1989, 1959 and back again to the present.

—from The Port Angeles Papers, *The Tower Echoes*, 1999.

On the Eiffel Tower in Paris there is now a giant electronic sign that is counting down the days, hours, minutes and seconds until the last midnight of the present century and the first moments of the next.

As I come to write something for the *Tower Echoes* it occurs to me that this will be the last time for me to reflect on the changing year for this newsletter. When "Y2K" [the year 2000] comes around, I will no longer be your pastor, but be retired or serving elsewhere. So what can we say now about such things?

The church is a community of memory and hope. I would like to share with you some reflections I had on such matters exactly ten years ago in which I quoted from my journal some forty years ago. I invite you to look back with me as I remembered and found hope in the face of the awesome dangers of the century that is passing. Maybe it will help us to confront the opportunities and hazards of the new millennium that is soon upon us. So, venturing into my past thoughts let me share:

We Are Still Here!!! Some Tales of Monks and Ducks

Near the end of the old year, I read a novel about the end of the world. It was published in 1959, and was about an order of monks founded by a Jewish scientist and weapons expert named Leibowitz who discovered the futility of war too late to stop it, became a Christian, survived a nuclear holocaust, and founded a monastic order that would preserve what was left of human learning for future generations he thought might one day want to be "civilized" again. In the "Simplification" that followed that holocaust, simple folk shot him through the head with an arrow. [They did that with everyone who "knew" anything in those days, because it was the "learned" and the "mighty" who brought the "deluge of fire" on the world.]

The novel opens after a long Dark Age, and the monastery in the desert has kept the light of learning alive faithfully all those generations in the name of their beloved founder. 1200 years went by and on the basis of this learning men struggled to acquire knowledge and science and technology again. The novel, A *Canticle for Leibowitz*, ends with *another* nuclear holocaust, and the world is at last consumed in fire as the human race destroys itself for trivial political reasons. Meanwhile a starship full of monks, nuns and children takes the faithfully preserved heritage of human knowledge, safely stored on microfilm, outward with them on a long voyage toward a distant galaxy, where the human adventure can begin anew.

This was once called "science fiction." Now, like laser guns . . . it may well be a scenario for tomorrow. And so, I found myself reading this novel some thirty years after it was written, and in the closing hours of 1988 observed that the world is still here.

Near the beginning of the New Year of our Lord 1989, I was browsing through my *Edinburgh Papers*—a journal I kept for a couple years while a student in Scotland. I found this:

"Tues. . . . Passing Princes Street Gardens, near St. John's Church, saw a mother duck with six little ducklings. . . . In the face of all the wear and tear and ruin and devastation and blind destructiveness . . . and the fragile tenure of things . . . these appear on the scene. A mockery of our attempts to destroy creation. Six baby ducklings, flaunting their existence at the great trend toward NOTHING we are in. . . . Meeting the whole hydrogen bomb-stupid world with a sensible: QUACK! Q U A C K ! . . . a loud and sensible . . . Q U A C K ! Six little ducklings and their Mom . . . quacking: "WE ARE!" to the world!

—from The Edinburgh Papers, *Edinburgh Journal*, 1959.

This too was written about thirty years ago, around the time the Soviets set off a massive hydrogen bomb in the Russian Arctic that altered the air pressure in Scotland for over fifteen minutes. What I referred to then as "the fragile tenure of things" is still very fragile—perhaps more so—*but . . . we are . . . still here!*

The world always seems to be ending. *But we are still here!* As 1989 opens there are some awesome tales of terrorism and chemical weapons and "retaliation." People saying "we believe in an eye for an eye," i.e., revenge . . . calling itself "justice." How about a "world" for a "world"? We haven't learned a whole lot since the Stone Age. The novel I read was only a "novel." Any truth in fiction? The ducks I saw were in fact only ducks. Any truth in ducks? Or in "facts"? Fact and fiction . . . like faith

. . . all seem to tell us . . . "The wages of sin is death." Can we also discover that the free gift of God is . . . "life" and that eternal? We can destroy this beautiful planet . . . We can't destroy God . . . who sent us Christ . . . and some noisy ducks . . . and faithful novelists with cautionary tales.

A New Year lies before us—full of possibilities. *We are still here!* As we begin again—"the fragile tenure of things" is still endangered by our selfish use and waste and pride and sinfulness. By our expertise in "blind destructiveness." The world is full of *senseless* "quacks." We need more ducks! Noisy, quacking ducks! Flocks of them! An epiphany of *sensible* Q U A C K S! to you!!!

—from Hutch . . . Your Pastor, Epiphany 1989—from The Palouse Papers, *The Messenger*, 1989.
—and forward again to The Port Angeles Papers, *The Tower Echoes*, 1999.

And now, a New Year . . . 1999, lies before *us*, and in addition, we soon face the Year of our Lord 2000, and a whole New Century. All of it is full of challenge, opportunity, and possibilities for both disaster and deliverance. Are there signs of hope?

Have you heard? Some pelicans . . . have suddenly appeared today . . . down by the pier! Right here, in the "Port of the Angels"! And did you know that the pelican . . . is an ancient symbol . . . of Christ???!!! A glad "epiphany" to you!

And finally, now, back to where we started . . . into the new millennium . . . and the year of our Lord 2004 . . . on the eve of the birthday celebration of a nation built on hope. May we remember who we are and where we came from and seek to renew those things that made us great, and amend those things that endanger our life together and with the world in which we live. The new millennium has come and appears to be as threatening as the last century. We can do better . . . and may God help us to do so.

There Are Names

How shall we be known?
And what shall we call ourselves?
Or others . . . like our kids, our pets,
An era, or a place . . .
We struggle sometimes to designate things . . .
And then exclaim . . .
"Ah well . . . what's in a name anyway?"
As perhaps a way of opting out . . . to anonymity.
Or, we may be apt to say . . .
"You name it! It's your call . . ."
As if our input made all the difference.

A child's name is heard
Before the child could
Even know it has a name.
This name is called
Until that delightful day
The child discovers that the name it hears
Is indeed its own . . .
And answers to the call.

I have known names that seem to sing;
Like Illimani—Crianlarich—
Senayan—Aberystwyth—Kitsilano—
Achnacarry—Coeur d'Alene . . .
And names no one can even say,
Like whatever they call that town in Wales which claims it has the
     longest name in all the world.

Some names shout to the sky
Of outrage and disaster,
Odious names the world would
Like to forget . . .
Names like Auschwitz, My Lai,
Or Heartbreak Hill.
Names that name a ghetto
Or a grave,
A place of nameless faces
Or of faceless names.
Names that should be forgotten but are not,
And names that ought to be remembered,
But that never will.

Often names are dropped
Into conversations;
To impress, or warn,
Imply a bribe,
Or even to console.
Others give way to nicknames
Or acronyms, like bureaucratic titles
Designed to ease our memories
And tax them even more.

Now and then a name
Becomes a destiny . . .
The name appears, and lives are changed,
A history happens
Bringing greatness or disaster
Until one day that name itself
Bestows a meaning,
Shapes events,
Or is descriptive of an Age:
Periclean–Elizabethan–Orwellian.

There are names that come to mind
In dreams,
On a dark stair,
In lonely rooms,
Or in the din of traffic.
There are names we say in hope,
Or offer up in prayer.
Names that haunt us,
Names that bless us . . .
Names that gladden all our days.

Some names
Recall the inventions of brilliant men . . .
Like the Eiffel Tower,
Morse's code,
Or Newton's laws.
And there are those that tell
A Mother's sorrow . . . like *Pieta,*
An enigmatic smile . . . the *Mona Lisa.*
Names that name a music,
Convey a mood, or state of mind;
Like a requiem, or blues,
A *Song of Love,*
The *Ode to Joy.*

Countless names have been placed
Upon the land . . .
To designate a mountain or a stream,
A quiet valley, or a lonely pass.
Names that describe a land that goes on forever . . . like Serengeti,
Or crown a continent . . . like Kilimanjaro
Holding up the sky with
All its snows.
And there are names of dear familiar streets,
Or cities that have charmed us:
Venice, and Vancouver—
Edinburgh—Lisbon—Rio—
Siena—and La Paz.

Know it or not,
We *are* our names.
And the way you say my name
Has made me claim it for myself,
And come to love it too.
Your name has now been present
In this exotic place whose name
I didn't even know until today.
It is as if you made the journey here yourself,
Shared this meal and met these friends,
Or saw trees blossom in all their glory
Beside this waterfall and quiet lake.

Today there is a name
That was but a number,
An early autumn date,
Or what one dials to summon aid in time of need.
But now this number/name
Re-tells a time of terror
When the towers fell,
As need and date,
And aid and number
Were fused by fire into a tearing
Numbness we cannot forget,
An ache within the heart,
A searing vision on the mind.

And then there is that Name
That has the claim to be
Above every other name,
Yet closer than hands or feet,
That dwells within the heart of those
Who love it
And causes knees to bend
In homage, and tongues to praise the name
Unspeakable . . .
The name of One

In whose name we get our names,
Who names our peace
And knows and writes
Our names within
"The Book of Life."

—from A Word in Season.

The Edinburgh Papers

Meetings in Mid-Atlantic

The Dutch Priest

We met, I believe, at the ship's rail, watching the wind play with the waves and send the sea birds soaring, as we enjoyed the fresh air and the warm sun, and the hum of the great engines below enabling our journey across the vast ocean. We then fell into a conversation and I discovered that he was a priest from the Netherlands. He was given passage to New York and back to Rotterdam on this Holland-America Lines vessel in return for conducting Mass on Sundays in the ship's chapel. He had never been to America before and got to stay a couple of weeks between sailings. I asked him what he thought of our country and he said he was really impressed with the churches he had visited in New York and Boston and Washington, D.C. He found them full of worshippers, and this both surprised and delighted him.

"What good are full churches," I said, "if people don't truly understand why they are there?" I then informed him that I was a theological student and was returning to Edinburgh where I was also serving in parishes of the Church of Scotland, and that I was equally as impressed with European theology as he was with American churches.

"What good is all that theology," he said, "if there is no faith in the people? If no one is in church, how will they come to believe it?"

50

"But just attending church," I said, "doesn't mean that the faith people have is informed by the theology of the church, and can be just a blind trust that is easily exploited or misguided in harmful ways."

"Theology can just be an academic exercise if there is no community like the church for it to find expression among the people and strengthen their faith," he observed.

Suddenly we both laughed. We each pondered the question the other had posed, and decided it was a good thing that we had met and were having this conversation. For we both realized afresh that it is equally important to *be* and to *believe,* to *belong* and to *know,* and to share together in the faith that we seek to understand, and to come to understand the faith that we seek to share.

I often wonder if that Dutch priest remembers our conversation with a sense of gratitude as I do. I kind of think he does. May our churches grow in numbers as they grow in understanding. And may they grow in understanding as they grow in numbers. To be "vital disciples" we must learn the faith. And to learn the faith we must learn it together. Only then can we bear witness to the need of the world in a loving and helpful way.

The Church is a Community of Vision. "*Where there is no vision the people perish.*" And, we might add, where there are no people the vision dies.

Come, let us see it together!

—Edinburgh, 1962

The Palouse Papers

On the Wings of the Morning Flight to Argentina

Sunday morning . . . we were not in church as usual, but at the airport . . . in Lima, Peru. We boarded a great jetliner and settled into our seats awaiting take-off. Suddenly the stewardess announced that there was a "medical emergency" and that we must all debark from the plane until further notice. Somewhat mystified, we dutifully unfastened our seat belts and returned via the exit ramp to the departure lounge of the airport.

Soon, the passengers, puzzled by the turn of events, began to speak to each other, speculating as to the nature of the emergency that caused the delay. While awaiting further word, we each began to tell our stories of where we were from and where we were going as strangers suddenly got acquainted. In our little gathering was a tractor salesman from England; a businessman from Lima enroute to Chile for a skiing vacation; and a young couple returning to Argentina from Peru after visiting family. They had a tiny dog, tucked away in a basket, which was brought out to entertain us. We talked and laughed and waited and wondered together about the reasons for the long delay and when the plane would finally be cleared for departure to Santiago and Buenos Aires. Someone observed that an elderly man had boarded the plane with his wife and may have had a heart attack or a stroke.

When the call finally came and we boarded the flight again we were aware that a death had occurred, and though we never did see the removal of the body, we had watched through the airport windows while some luggage was unloaded from the plane and taken away, followed by a sorrowing woman. The passengers were now a somewhat somber group whose quiet words to each other differed remarkably from the lively conversations that had developed over the past hour or so.

We then learned the delay was caused by the need to get the authorities out to verify the circumstances of the man's death. There was a shared hush among the passengers. A death had occurred of a man that none of us knew. But that man's dying had brought us together. We were no longer strangers. We shared a sorrow, and a sense of the fragile finitude of things, but were strangely grateful for having met each other. Then the engines roared and the great plane taxied out to the runway and took off on its journey across the continent.

I think we were somewhere over Bolivia when the captain's voice came over the intercom. Speaking with a quiet authority, in Spanish and then in English, he said gently, "My friends, I don't have to explain much to you about what has happened this morning . . . I'm sure you are all aware . . . but I would only ask . . . that in your prayers today . . . you would remember Raoul."

It was a moment of worship. Here we were . . . skipping church to catch a flight . . . and yet . . . called to prayer . . . by a pilot of the national airline of Peru. A death had taken place that had made a passenger list of strangers a community of memory and hope, and now that gathered community was called to solemn intercession as they journeyed on together. I was reminded of Karl Barth's great word . . . "the Church *is* . . . where it takes place." The "Church" took place that Sunday morning high over the Andes as the great jetliner carried its congregation toward their several destinies and into the higher Presence of the One who brings life and community out of death and departure.

Is this not indeed an image of the church? Do we not come from many places and find ourselves on a journey together? Is it not true that we meet because of One we did not know, who died to bring us together? And though we meet as strangers, can we not come to know one another because of him, and tell our stories and share our lives and pray for each other and depart as friends?

Come! . . . let us worship God! . . . and in your prayers today . . . "remember Raoul."

—from *The Messenger*, Simpson United Methodist Church, Pullman, Washington, 1990.

The Palouse Papers

Why Not Pro-Love?

Dan Quayle, bless him, blew it! He said something like how he would support his daughter whatever her decision regarding an unwanted pregnancy! "Pro-lifers" are outraged. Conservatives feel betrayed. "Pro-choicers" are perplexed. Liberals wish he hadn't said it. "Surely," all agree, "Dan Quayle must be a bit confused!" So, what else is new? Wife, Marilyn Quayle, jumped in with "damage control." Too late.

It was the best thing he ever said, in my opinion. It was the candid word of a father, not the "politically correct" utterance of a Vice President or a political candidate. It expressed the value of his family to him, not his "family values." And he said it about the hottest topic in the land and the one that continually threatens to tear the nation apart.

As citizens we seem to be confronted with choices regarding the abortion issue that don't seem capable of resolution in the political arena. Probably because they are not. I, for one, am tired of the sound and the fury. The media bombard us with the news of clinics attacked and "Missions to the unborn," of rights defended and rights denied. We all receive phone calls and petitions to sign and letters *ad nauseum* on both sides of the abortion issue. Believers in passing or defeating initiatives or defeating or electing candidates on whether or not they support their cause, view their cause as a life or death matter. They are right. Literally.

At risk of being regarded as "politically incorrect" by all concerned, I must nevertheless assert my frustration with both sides. I realize that when we go to the polling booth we are going to have to decide between what the ballot on that day offers us as new legislation and/or legislators and what the *status quo* exhibits with respect to this important issue. This is a very important decision and *we can't escape the responsibility of deciding on the specifics of the options placed before us.*

The choices will be political ones that day. Yet they reflect the complex of values, secular and religious, that makes up the warp and woof of the national fabric. These threads are so interwoven into our national life that it is hard to sort them out. And so we tend to want to simplify it beyond all complexity and decide it as if life could be reduced to a single issue. The result is not simple, but simplistic.

So how are we, not only as citizens, but also as believers of one sort or another, to decide such important matters?

The great American theologian, Reinhold Niebuhr, often warned against a "shallow consistency" in our thinking and acting on complex issues like this. I believe both sides in this life and death issue are guilty of such a "shallow consistency." Both sides of the issue of abortion have truth on their side. Both sides, it seems to me, commit fundamental errors of judgment that lead to charges hurled at each other in this tragic conflict of values.

And it is, indeed, a conflict of values, not just a question of law. We value life. We value freedom. Is there not an ethical way of understanding that values both? And would like to see both protected by the law in our land? There is! It is basic to our roots from which we derive our values. It is in our great biblical heritage and faith.

The *summum bonum,* or "highest good" as far as Christian ethics as been able to articulate it . . . is *Love.* Not Life. Not Freedom. Love. *Freedom and Life are subordinate to Love.* We are to "love God with all our heart and soul and mind and strength." To love God . . . above all other gods, goods, or values. Including "Life" and "Freedom." And we are to "love our neighbor as ourselves." Love respects the life of others and honors their freedom. And all of this together . . . at the same time!

Love has to make terrible choices on behalf of life and freedom. Love takes responsibility for life, and for freedom. It does not hide behind a law that decides such matters. When confronted with matters of life and death, blessing and cursing, it chooses life. But notice, it CHOOSES life. It chooses LIFE! It chooses life for LOVE'S sake, not for Life's sake or for Freedom's sake nor for Law's sake.

Love recognizes the complexities of the human predicament. It knows that life is a blessing and that freedom is a responsibility. But it also *knows that life can become a curse and freedom an excuse and refuses to make an idol out of either.* It affirms both and caters to neither.

Biblically speaking, to regard life, or freedom, as an absolute is to fall into idolatry. *The problem Love recognizes is that to choose life or freedom sometimes means death to someone. Love maximizes both life and freedom and will also sacrifice both for Love.*

Shall we say it again? Love will sacrifice life and/or freedom for love's sake. It is an awesome and tragic and terrible choice that cannot be resolved merely by law and yet respects the values that law seeks to serve. We cannot absolve ourselves of moral responsibility by legal means. We cannot decide the ultimate issues of life merely at the ballot box. The law can protect, regulate, clarify, express and implement but it cannot determine your moral status by making your decisions for you.

Life is a "gift" before it is a "right." And so is freedom. We can only be "pro-choice" and "pro-life" by being "pro-love." And then we will be both, realizing that our moral choices can't be reduced to legal or political options. The dilemma of life is real. To sacrifice freedom for the sake of life, or life for the sake of freedom, does not resolve the dilemma. It only intensifies it.

And it is a real dilemma, awesome in its implications. Attempts to resolve it have led to promulgations of doctrine or enactments of law that seek to preserve either life or freedom in the face of impending violence that would destroy either. The *Doctrine of the Just War* was formulated to address this in conflict among nations. *Roe vs. Wade* was legislated to address this with regard to problems of human generation. Both seek to limit violence and preserve freedom.

I think Dan Quayle spoke out of an awareness of this dilemma. Not as a Vice-President, but as a father. Like most people, I would shudder to think of him as the President of the United States. But I think that perhaps as a dad, he has given us cause to be proud of him.

We have to decide for ourselves what is right, in the light of the values and laws and circumstances in which our lives are lived. Including at the ballot box! Ponder these things . . . and try to vote responsibly on Election Day. Not to decide is to decide. To decide is to decide. Seek to do the *loving* thing for all involved. We have set before us life and death . . . therefore we must choose.

The Vancouver Papers
Sent: August 4, 2004

A Sonnet to One Who Still Loves Us

If we could love the Love that still loves us,
And still the love that loves in vain,
Then we would love the world that you love still,
And not those things that cause you pain.
Could we care for you as you care for all,
And all would care, and not care less,
Then might not all our caring count for more,
And more would know your world is blessed?
If we believed the word you came to share,
And shared the truth that sets us free,
Then the world would know of your love and care

And love the world you want to be.
        Lord, help us to care for the world we share,
        And free us to love the ones in our care.

> —from A *Word in Season*. Written in a class with Madeleine L'Engle at Vancouver School of Theology, Summer 1995. Editor's Choice Award for Outstanding Achievement in Poetry, March 2004, International Library of Poetry.

Sacred Humanism and a Secular Faith?

A really lively topic of discussion on this campus is "secular humanism," which has been attacked for its "godless" character, and deplored as a substitute faith that is being taught in our public schools and universities. Those attacking "secular humanism" often do so in the name of "Christianity."

Conversely, "secular humanism" has been defended for its "objectivity" and open approach to truth. Those defending "secular humanism" extol its virtues of humility and open-mindedness; free from the narrow-minded bias of "true believers."

We at the Common Ministry see in the Christian faith an alternative to this "no win" dispute. If the gospel of Jesus Christ is true, we cannot embrace a humanism devoid of transcendence. Nor can we believe in a pietism bereft of humanity. Why?

The problem we see with "secular humanism" is not that it is evil or godless, but that it is too timid. There are more things in heaven and earth than are dreamt of in this philosophy.

The problem we see with a "Christianity" devoid of humanism is that it is too arrogant. It seeks to opt out of the human predicament by a faith stance that forgets that the heart of the Christian message is "the Word made flesh." . . . . God coming to us as a carpenter from Nazareth, a man who must die at the hands of religious men doing their duty to God.

It is possible to be a humanist and not be a Christian. But one cannot be a Christian and not also be a humanist. The predicament we face is that we either want a sure and simple faith, secure from the threat of human frailty and fallibility—or we want a sophisticated world view or philosophy, free from the threat of some sort of a supernatural form of transcendence.

We seem to want a *sacred faith* or a *secular humanism.*

Maybe instead, we need a *sacred humanism* and a *secular faith?*

In fact, that is what we have in the New Testament, where we read of One of whom it is said that he is both the Son of God and the Son of Man. Jesus Christ is the meeting place of time and eternity, God and humanity, the *secular* and the *sacred.* In him we meet a man who speaks to us as God, and a God who confronts us in this man. In him we see "the human face of God," and the ultimate dignity of humanity.

No philosophy or religion in the world has a higher esteem for that which is human. Likewise, no philosophy or religion in the world has a more secular or worldly view of the divine.

In the gospel of Jesus Christ we are presented with a faith that is all bound up with the world. We are informed that the living God loves this world, our world, to the very death. In Jesus Christ, a crucified and risen Lord confronts us with a *sacred humanity* and the *humanity of God.* We are given a faith not *of* the world, but *for* the world, by which we are summoned to live *in* the world . . . this world . . . that God created and loves and will transform into a "new heaven and a new earth, in which righteousness dwells."

—from *The Common Ministry,* September 28, 1987 and *The Evergreen,* the Washington State University daily newspaper.

The Port Angeles Papers, 1996 and The Jakarta Journal, 2000

A Time for Teamwork

We live in a house of broken clocks. One clock can tell the time but not proclaim it. Another can do neither. The first, the "Nana" clock, can chime the quarter hours but not the hour. The second, a mantel clock purchased for $3.50 at a rummage sale, ran perfectly for six or seven years and then gave up. A repairman last year kept it for six months and then charged us $102 to fix it. This "repair" lasted less than a week. Now it is frozen in time at 7:05, whether AM or PM we'll let you decide! [When we packed it away in our basement to go to Jakarta . . . it suddenly started to work again! It was funny to hear it chiming away behind all those boxes!]

If an International Olympics were held for clocks, ours wouldn't qualify! This leads me to the observation that clocks are a kind of team. It takes teamwork to tell the time. It takes time to develop teamwork. Neither a clock nor a team can do their stuff if the parts don't work together. It takes skill and/or money to fix a clock, or field a team. How about a church? Or a world?

It is amazing how we take clocks for granted! We don't even notice them when they are working, except of course when we need to know the time—when they are broken, however, we *hear* their silence—and when they can't tell the time they annoy us.

The Olympics are almost over and coming again. All that teamwork and time of preparation and performance, the winning and the losing. Sports are that way. We remember "Mariner fever" last year! The Seattle Mariners are still playing but in a slump. Even a championship team cannot always win. Perhaps the world is full of broken clocks and losing teams!

A church is a team. It takes time and teamwork to be the Church. Notice! . . . *Team! Work!* Let's not take the Church for granted! *You,* like all other members of this congregation, are needed to participate. Imagine a clock with no hands or chimes to proclaim the time! This team we call Church is not a spectator sport, even if the whole world is watching.

A clock team tells the time. A church is a team to proclaim the "eternities." In a timely way! This takes time, teamwork, resources; therefore commitment and conviction. We can give our cash, but all the money in the world won't do the job if we don't work together. Think of the time, commitment and cost of the Olympic Games! And more teams lost than won!

Here the analogies break down. A clock, as ours demonstrate, can't work if there are broken parts. A team can hardly win if there are injured players. But the church can prevail with broken people.

But if a church is a team of broken people, how can it "get the

Gold?" *The Church is the people who already have the Gold!* We won the loser's Olympics! We, like our Coach, are "wounded healers!" Some things only the broken can fix! Some things only losers can understand . . . like a wounded, broken, loser world that needs compassion and "the fellowship of those who bear the mark of pain." Those who have failed appreciate the true meaning of success—the real joy of victory—the glory of a united effort where we share our losses and maximize our gains. A *real team* knows this. Just a bunch of losers doesn't, and can turn even victory into defeat, success into failure.

The Church is and can and must be a real team. In Christ we are "members one of another" and therefore willing and able to help each other along our common way. Let's go for the Gold! Let's show how to run the human race!

Anybody know how to fix a clock?

—from "A View from the Tower," *The Tower Echoes*, First United Methodist Church, Port Angeles, Washington, August 1996 and *The Jakarta Community Church News*, Jakarta, Indonesia, April 2000.

The Palouse Papers

Holy Clutter

I am sitting in Jim Watson's office up at the "K-House" waiting for the Common Ministry Council meeting to begin. I welcome the time to put down some ideas for *The Messenger* of how we are into the exciting frenzy of the year's activities in our church and university and town, but conclude you know that already! So what are we so busy with at the church in this place and time?

I look about me and I notice . . . ahem, shall we say . . . the . . . uh . . . clutter of a colleague's desk! [Kind of like mine, Watson, but I have a "Chremlin" that tidies it up when I'm not looking!] My eye falls upon some books. First, I see *Habits of the Heart* by Robert N. Bellah et al . . .

the noted sociological study of civil religion in America, and its roots in biblical faith and the republican traditions of Classical culture. In front of this book is another, *The Bible Makes Sense*, by Walter Brueggemann, and closest to me is *The Good News Bible in English*. Off to the right and toward the back of the desk . . . half covered by some papers, is *Lest Innocent Blood Be Shed*, by Phillip Hallie, the story of the brave Christians of Le Chambon sur Lignon in France, who saved hundreds of French Jews from the pogroms of the Third Reich in World War II. Half hidden by this book is another, with stars on the cover called *Genesis: A Book of Beginnings*, a commentary on the first book of the Bible. Finally, off to the back of the desk is a newsletter of the Inter-Faith Action Committee for Economic Justice. All of this under the watchful eyes of an Orthodox icon of the head of Christ and those of a picture of Jim's kids, Zachary and Annika, above the desk.

So here it is—not just the clutter of our campus ministry colleague's desk. There before my eyes are the symbols of what we are about as the church in the world and in this place called Pullman, and at the heart of this university. These are signs and symbols and tools of a whole ministry in a broken world. A holy ministry in a profane world. A healing ministry in a sick and often sickening world. It begins with Genesis, the book of Beginnings. It becomes the Good News . . . the Word of God to us in our own speech and syntax . . . that we may read it and hear it and do it. This book—this Bible—takes a lot of study and interpretation, and then we discover it makes sense—wonderful sense of our world and situation, and does indeed become God's Word to us from the Beginning, and for the Now, and to the End. Out of it we form those "habits of the heart" that make civilized life possible. That call individuals into a life of commitment to and with each other—that there might be justice, economic and otherwise—as well as compassion and daring, and faith—"lest innocent blood be shed."

A holy clutter! A whole and holy and healing ministry. In a broken and profane and unwell world. That is why we are here! Here, where even in a university town life doesn't always make sense. But the Bible does. Its great Word comprehends our wordiness. Its words tell of the Word we need to hear, that we might find healing for our malaise, and a holy Presence that leads us on. What a calling! What a task! What a privilege! Thanks Jim . . . for letting me use your office! And thanks too . . . for the holy clutter!

"Hutchins" Your clutzy cluttered colleague!

—from *The Messenger*, Simpson United Methodist Church, Pullman, Washington, September 1988.

The 9/11 Papers—V

In war, truth is the first casualty.

—Aeschylus, 525-456 BC

A couple of days after the awesome and horrendous events of September 11, I encountered a friend in the grocery store checkout line. I said to him, "It's a new world, Jeff." He responded immediately . . . "It had better be . . . " This has haunted me ever since . . . this simple and brilliant, yet demanding assessment of the crisis of the world since 9/11.

It had better be a New World. And yet we seem to be responding in the same old ways . . . with actions more akin to the abuse of power than the wisdom of discernment. We want to cry out . . . to get even . . . to "do something" . . . to respond to our hurt with harm to the evil perpetrators of such terrible deeds. News program platforms on television have titles like "America Strikes Back" . . . We want to divide the world into enemies we can destroy and friends we can count on . . . rather than seeing it for the broken world it is . . . where today's enemies were yesterday's friends and vice versa. I read yesterday where our government sent a 73 million dollar check to the Taliban last May. They were our "friends" then. And not too long ago our current ally, President Putin of Russia, was being described as "the butcher of Chechnya."

A couple of days ago, on CNN, I heard the Defense Secretary say we had now dropped three huge bombs on Afghanistan . . . bombs the size of a Volkswagen . . . bombs called "Daisy Killers" . . . bombs that incinerate everything within 600 yards of impact . . . that's 1,800 feet . . . six football fields. To his credit, the Secretary described them bluntly but honestly as bombs that are meant to "kill people." Simultaneously, at the bottom of the screen, where the latest news flashes by . . . were the words, "President Bush says we are not targeting civilians." But then, I guess we are supposed to understand that soldiers, being non-civilians, are not "people." . . . at least enemy soldiers. The truth is soldiers and civilians are all "people." There were civilians killed in the Pentagon. There were probably soldiers in the World Trade Center. They are all dead people.

What is wrong with this picture? This is not a "new" world . . . A political cartoon recently portrayed it better than I can . . . It showed Uncle Sam confronted with a huge serpent labeled "Terrorism" and he said something like . . . "We can take care of this" . . . as he chopped it into pieces with a giant axe . . . each one of which immediately sprouted the head of a new serpent turning to strike him.

A professional mediator in international conflict recently described what we are doing is "like hitting a dandelion with a golf club."

I met a man . . . recently from Afghanistan . . . where he and his wife worked with an Aid Program for the people there . . . who affirmed that we are doing exactly what Osama bin Laden wants us to do: getting into a war that can be manipulated into a "Holy War" between "Islam" and the "West." In such a war, there will be a lot more casualties than truth.

It had better be a "New World" . . . However, it doesn't look like it is . . .

What would a "new" and different "world" look like?

Maybe it is time to seek "The Next War" . . . *where each proud fighter brags he wars on death for lives . . . not men for flags.*

—Wilfred Owen, killed in action in WWI, 1918.
—from *The 9/11 Papers*, September 2001.

Augustine

He was the child of a mother's
    tears and prayers,
This poet of the restless heart,
Who gave us conscience and confession.
Wrestling the grave temptations
    that torment us all,
He charted well the anguished seas

of inwardness,
A subtle cartographer of the soul.

How well he knew the selfish city
        with its backward streets,
        snares and delights,
All alleyways of shame,
        and cul-de-sacs of meaning;
Unruly affections, lusts of the flesh,
        and the pride of life;
Until, subdued at last
        by emanations of a holy love,
He heard a voice calling to him from the garden . . .
        took up the book to read,
And sensed God's dazzling City . . .
        even in the decadence of Rome.

Announcing the vision of its bliss
        to generations yet unborn,
He defended it against the accusations
        of rebellious pride.
When the cities of empire fell
        to the barbarian hordes,
        he was an aged bishop in a seaport town,
        upon his knees at prayer.
The world that he had known was ended,
        and the grace that found him
        just begun.

"O Lord, you have made us for yourself . . ."

—from A Word in Season.

A Humble Prayer

History belongs to the intercessors, who believe the future into being.

—Walter Wink

We live in a secular, materialistic, alienated and competitive world of strangers. A world where many people do not believe in prayer, do not pray, and would not want to be caught dead trying. A world that seems to be too proud to pray.

Last Saturday while at the church for a pre-marriage consultation, a young man came by to make a request of me. He said he was from out of town, and was emotionally distraught and wanted me to pray with him. Thinking he might need to talk as well, I asked if he could wait a few minutes until I finished speaking with the couple in my office. When they left, I invited him in.

He explained again his predicament, including a history of struggle with mental illness, asked if I was indeed the Pastor, requested again that I pray with him, and then announced that he would pray first. He launched into an earnest prayer for divine help in his struggle for a "sound" mind and a tranquil spirit. Here was one whose need was so great he needed to pray about it. His prayer was totally for himself. And yet it was a humble prayer. He needed others to pray with him and for him and was not too proud to acknowledge that fact. He closed his prayer and then I took his hand and prayed for him, asking that he be granted a new awareness of God's gracious presence and help, and be freed to be concerned for others who need a friend. We finished, and he graciously thanked me for my time and intercession and left.

I went from there to the hospital to pray again, this time with a dying woman and her daughter watching by her bed.

All of these people I had barely met, and yet they are now close companions in my memory. How often have I witnessed this reality, and yet it never ceases to amaze me. Strangers are embraced in an intimacy that is as astonishing as it is real. People suddenly find themselves within a New World where there is comfort in sorrow, strength in weakness, order out of chaos, new purpose where all seemed lost, and a profound intimacy in human relationships.

Prayer is, indeed, the instant transformation of the world, by those who dare to "believe the future into being." Let us pray—the world, and we, are in need of it.

—from *The Messenger*, Simpson United Methodist Church, Pullman, Washington, September 1990.

The Palouse Papers

Ode to Outrage: At the Impending Election—1988

Cry out!
Rage!
Shout "Foul!"

Outrage!
Livid offspring of the
    anguished world,
    fume retribution
    for offended justice!
Sting with rebuke
    insensible hordes
    of callous indifference!
Let the odor of rage
    stink to high heaven,
    like the error sols eating
    the ozone.
Acid the rain on the muck ridden beaches
    of the cesspool whale eating sea!

The beggars for bread,
    eating budgets of lead, turn to
    mountains of dead;
While the polls for the pols,
    to see who's ahead,
    palls the contest for power,
    the election of dread.
Ennui wins
    in this candidate's carnival,
    the sequels of sound-bytes
    and rip-off of rhetoric
Are the rape of our reason
    in the lies we are fed.

Cry outrage!
Time of terror
    and tears
Tearing time!
Cry out! Rage!
Cry outrage!
Do not go gentle into
    this bad night,
But rage, rage!
Cry!
Outrage!

For the light.

—from A Word in Season.

This poem was begun while attending a concert at the Washington-Idaho Symphony after watching the evening news about one of the most vicious elections I had ever experienced. In the poem are reflected some of the context elements of that impending election.

For example, the lines "like the error sols eating the ozone" reflect the reports at the time of the increased depletion of the ozone layer in the atmosphere due to the widespread use of aerosol sprays.

The lines "acid the rain on the muck ridden beaches of the cesspool whale eating sea" . . . reflect the news regarding the pollution of both the air and the seas that were even then killing whales in the Arctic Ocean.

Much of the rest of the poem could probably be written about the current election . . . Especially the lines about "beggars for bread . . . eating budgets of lead . . . turn to mountains of dead . . .

We face a crisis that is immense . . . and calls for careful action . . . and frankly . . . once again and more than ever . . . outrage.

—from *The Messenger,* Simpson United Methodist Church, October 1988.

The Port Angeles Papers

On Loving Learning and Learning to Love

The boy was about eight to ten I guess, and wore a sweatshirt that proclaimed HOME SCHOOLING, and an Air Force officer's cap that probably belonged to his father, who looked like he might be retired military. They joined me in the customer's lounge at the automobile dealership where we were getting our cars serviced early on that morning.

They no sooner sat down than out of a rucksack came some books and a home schooling session began. The father would read from a book and often stop to interrogate his son as to his knowledge of the subject matter at the time. The boy was very bright and had good answers and excellent questions. So I sipped my coffee and listened with great interest. They even drew me into the conversation a couple of times.

They began with an American history lesson, and the discussion ranged from Thomas Jefferson and the Louisiana Purchase to the Lewis and Clark exploration of that vast territory [once, when the dad couldn't answer a question about Lewis and Clark he inquired of me what the answer might be]; and on to James Madison, "father of the Constitution," and how the streets of Washington D.C. were all mud when he and Dolly came to town; then it was on to the Alamo and the Mexican War, and the addition of the rest of the states to the Union. Suddenly the topic shifted to figures of speech, like, "better late than never," and then to World Geography. The boy identified where Tibet was to be found and asked questions of his dad about why China wants to keep it and got a bit of world history about the Burma Road and Chennault and the Flying Tigers in World War II. Then the topic shifted again and we were into Galileo and the telescope and how the Church gave him a bad time for expanding our view of the universe! Galileo had been reading Copernicus . . . [I wanted to throw in there how Copernicus had been *encouraged* in his scientific inquiries by the Church] but then suddenly I was informed that my car was ready and I had to leave. On my way out I said, "Thank you for the good lesson!"

It was a fascinating, serendipitous kind of happening! I was impressed. [Indeed, I remembered all those people during the war in Nicaragua that couldn't even locate it on the map, and yet this boy knew how to ask questions about Tibet!] I marveled at the wonderful interaction between the father and his son. Learning was valued. Personal relationships in the learning process were there to enhance the learning, and in the exchange of ideas and information a lot more was communicated than the subject matter. If it didn't make me a convert to home schooling it certainly reinforced the notion endorsed by the public schools as well that parents ought to be involved in their children's education. We have become all too aware of how deprived some children are for personal relationships of the parental kind that radically affect their learning ability and motivation. Besides, what a great way to teach the parents! It also reminded me of the time that I asked people in neighborhood "get acquainted" groups in a new parish to name who had influenced their lives more than anyone—and discovered that it was Sunday School teachers that won hands down. Why? Because, I was told, they cared about the kids and communicated more than the lesson. Indeed, the most effective lesson *was the teacher.*

Maybe this encounter I had with home schooling can be a lesson for us all, whether we are parents or grandparents, Church School teachers, or involved in education in the public schools. Maybe we all need to learn to "teach and admonish one another in all wisdom" . . . that we who teach and learn may all grow up to maturity by learning to "speak the truth in love."

Let us keep on learning and loving!

—from "The View from the Tower," *The Tower Echoes*, First United
Methodist and Congregational Church, Port Angeles, Washington 1994.

The Palouse Papers, 1989 and The Port Angeles Papers, 1995

Hanford Reservations

Near Vernita Bridge—where the Columbia River flows eastward on the "Hanford
Reach," and the Department of Energy signs forbid all access—and say:
    Arid Lands Ecology Reserve
    All Plants and Animals Protected
    U.S. Atomic Energy Commission

Ask the sagebrush now to tell
What the river carried
In its waters to the sea.
Ask the river or the sun
What strange things were here begun,
What they all could well
Reveal, having witnessed what was done.

Here the mighty river's run
On its westward journey to the sea,
Reaches toward the rising sun . . .
Does it turn to seek its source again
From where it witnessed what was done?
All the strange things here begun?
Ask the river in its run,
Falling toward the rising sun.

In this wasteland of the sage
We turned as well . . . though
Not to seek our Source beyond the gentle dawn.
Reaching out in fear, we fell . . . and

Split the very substance of the sun itself—
Exploding light—that brought this night
With flags of danger now unfurled,
Refusing us all access
To the quiet evening of the world.

Ask the wasted sage to tell,
Or the river in its run,
What strange things were here begun,
And what it was we thought we'd won.
What they all could now reveal
And how they witnessed what was done . . .
Ask the Land of the Rising Sun.

Ask the sage if it might tell,
Or the river how we fell,
Ask the sun that casts its spell
How we here gave birth to hell,
Ask yourselves as well . . .

Ask the sagebrush now to tell
Ask yourselves . . . as well.

—from *The Messenger,* Simpson United Methodist Church, Pullman,
Washington, January 1989.

TIDEPOOLS 1995—Port Angeles, Washington
A Word in Season —GRAHAM HUTCHINS

"The Hanford Nuclear Reservation is already the most contaminated site in
the Western Hemisphere." Statement from Initiative 297, Washington State
Voters Pamphlet, 2004.

Meetings in Mid-Atlantic

The Scientist from Paris

I can see him now, pacing the deck of the ship, his white hair whipped by the wind, and his face intent on discernment of the enigmas behind sea and sky. I don't believe he even noticed the view, his quest was for things unseen.

And then one day we happened to meet. I don't quite remember how, but something got us into a conversation. He didn't seem to talk to anyone else. I am still surprised he talked to me. Upon meeting we shared the usual amenities and our observations of the voyage. He told me he was a scientist, a geologist, and he had seen much of the world . . . from the Andes to Asia, and from the Australian Outback to the Canadian Rockies, and more. He was returning again to his home in Paris on this ship from New York and Boston to Rotterdam. I think he must have walked half the distance just pacing the deck. Then I told him I was returning to Edinburgh to resume my theological studies. He laughed, and looked at me as if he had seen a ghost. He found it incredible that anyone would study such an arcane and anachronistic subject matter as "theology."

"Would you study alchemy," he asked, "instead of chemistry?" "Or astrology, when there's astronomy and astrophysics?"

"Not at all," I replied. "Would you make a religion out of science?"

He looked at me with new respect, and we went on to have a very interesting philosophical conversation. I remember it ended with him asserting that the only religion he had ever seen that was in any way attractive to him was on the island of Bali. All the rest was so much fantasy and superstition, and he wanted no part of it. And then he was off to pace the deck once again.

Several times more when we encountered one another he would give me a polite nod, but did not engage me in conversation. Then one day he approached me again, and we talked for awhile.

"You know, I have been watching you," I said finally, "and you bring to mind that great confessional statement of St. Augustine . . . '*O Lord, you have made us for yourself, and our hearts are restless until they find their rest in you.*' " He didn't laugh this time, but turned away to pace the deck some more.

The next day I disembarked at Southhampton. I never saw him again. And yet I can still see him . . . pacing the deck . . . looking for God . . . the God he can't believe in. I am consoled only by the fact that the God he can't believe in was looking for him. I hope they happened to meet one day, as we did, and had some good conversation . . . and went on their way together.

—from *Some Words for All Seasons*

Some Seasoned Words

We had hoped this
    would happen someday;
    longing in the dark yearning
    of a whimpering world,
    for Someone to present us
    with the unwrapped Presence
    of a holy love.
With radiant eyes,
    and something like
    a reckless devotion;
We followed foolishly,
    and wandered somewhere
    into wonder,
    toward a dark and Friday noon;
Hardly aware
    this was a lethal
    sort of preparation

for our journey
into joy.

We were rescued
        somehow
        by a lightning grace,
        and knew a grief eclipsed
        at sunrise;
For when this fire fell
        from heaven,
We found ourselves
        somewhat surprised
        to be Somebody
        who could wear this light
        like flesh,
        and have these tongues
        to tell our witness
        to the wailing world,
How Love calls forth a people,
        to be a City
        singing in the
        sun.

This is the first time I have included a poem from my book *Some Words for All Seasons* in the selections I have sent out on *Paper Trails*. . . . The book enables reflection on the themes of the liturgical and natural seasons as well as contemporary life. It consists of seven poems illustrated with many of my photographs that are coordinated with the poems. The book has been well received and many have found that it makes a fine gift for the holiday season. It is now available at **Amazon.com.** To access it, type **Amazon.com** on your browser address line, and when their website appears, select **Books,** and then on the search bar type in: **Some Words for All Seasons** and you will soon bring up the information about it. You can browse within the book there, and if you are familiar with it already can even write a review of it online, if you so desire.

It has been much appreciated by those who have read it—as have my *Paper Trails* that many of you have responded to over the past several

months. Thank you for letting me share my thoughts and faith with you
in these ways.

On Getting and Giving

We make a living by what we get, but we make a life by what we give.

—Winston Churchill

Thanksgiving is upon us again. That holiday when we as a people pause
to give thanks, even though we officially separate church and state.

We have built a nation in which we have celebrated hard work and
felt justified in the enjoyment of the fruits of our labor. We are "getters
and spenders" such as the world has never seen before. We have been so
busy and successful in our work that we often don't even feel the need to
stop and say "thanks" to anyone—let alone God.

The question arises. . . . While we have been so industrious in making a living by what we get, have we made a life for ourselves? Is not life
more than just survival? Do we not need skills just for living as much or
more than just for survival and providing? A means for life as well as for
livelihood? "We make a living by what we get," said Winston Churchill,
but how do we make a life?

"We make a life by what we give." Maybe this further word of Churchill's is good advice for us.

Is giving the opposite of getting? Or something different altogether? Maybe these are not opposites at all? The opposite of "getting"
might be "getting taken" in a competitive society like ours. The true opposite of "giving" might be "receiving." These might have more to do
with quality of life than with a quantity of things.

When we merely get and spend and get "took," we find cause neither for thanks nor for the real enjoyment of life. Greed can provoke

grudges. Or we get too proud in our "getting" . . . too confident in our own abilities to acknowledge our indebtedness or gratitude to others. We, and they, get only what we, or they "deserve." No less, no more. We get ahead, or we get taken. That's America. Is it? If so, it is very sad.

Thoreau once observed that most people lead lives of "quiet desperation." Does that describe our present mood as well? Except we are not so "quiet" about it. Perhaps our modern world is more characterized by lives of "shrill" desperation. If all we know is getting ahead, or getting "took," that is desperate.

There is a better way. When we give we receive, and we find reasons for thanksgiving. We learn how to give to others, and allow others to give to us. Could we not learn to give . . . and to receive? Might we learn to live lives of "quiet gratitude"? Someone in our past thought it possible, and in a secular society such as ours, nonetheless decided we ought to set aside at least one day in the year to pause in the busy rush of getting a living and take time to give thanks for all that we have received in our lives.

It may be true that "we make a living by what we get" . . . but it is also true that we "make a life by what we give." Let us learn again . . . to give . . . and to receive . . . and most of all . . . to give thanks.

—Graham Hutchins, Pastor, Simpson United Methodist Church, Pullman, Washington.

Hymn for Advent

Tune: Wer Nur Den Lieben Gott
99.98.88
#142 United Methodist Hymnal

1. O Lord the darkness cannot hide you.
Yet we your people long for light,
There is no hope for us without you,
We wander lost in gloom of night;
Come to us now, O Lord, we pray,

And warm our hearts with your new day.

2. O Lord in foolishness and pride,
The nations stumble on their way,
While walls of hate again divide,
And love is easy to betray;
O come, and dwell with us, O Lord,
And teach us from your living Word.

3. O God with us now come to dwell,
Bone of our bone and flesh appear,
In our own life yourself reveal,
Until our lives your image bear:
O God, be with us all this night,
And lead us gently to the light

4. O Light of Light, your radiance share,
Rise in our hearts, our minds and will,
Fill all our days with deeds of care,
Bid all our anxious fears be still;
O God of God, your glory show,
Be with us now, your grace to know.

—from Hymns for All Seasons, 1992.

The Gospel According to Spellcheck!

The Pastor was writing a message about how the Christmas season proclaims the amazing fact that "God is with us" and that this is the meaning of the title from Isaiah used by Matthew to describe Jesus . . . *Emmanuel.* He paused—is it *Emmanuel*? Or is it *Immanuel*? Both translations from the original Hebrew appear quite frequently. Hmm . . . time to use "spellcheck" . . . that amazing device that helps computer users to present documents free of some of the most embarrassing errors. A keystroke or two later the Pastor read the following:

"Emmanuel—there is no alternative for this."

Out of the mouths of babes and computers! PROCLAMATION!!! No alternative can be found for *"Emmanuel"*! Good ol' IBM! Marvelous Microsoft! God is with us indeed! Surprise! Surprise!

It reminded the Pastor of a series of sermons he wished he had preached . . . called *"Unwitting Witnesses."* They were about all the statements in the Gospels made by people trying to put Jesus down that really bore witness to him in a powerful way . . . like "he saved others, let him save himself" . . . bears witness that in saving others he was willing and able to do so. Or Pilate's cynical sign on the Cross that said, in three languages, *This is Jesus of Nazareth, King of the Jews.* Pilate meant it as a warning that in the Roman Empire this kind of bloody end is what happens to upstart revolutionaries or wannabe Messiahs, and poor stupid Pilate didn't realize that by putting it that way he really bore witness to the truth.

And so an unwitting witness appeared right before the Pastor's eyes on the screen of his computer. No alternative for *Emmanuel*! Amen! So he tried *Immanuel* . . . and "spellcheck" called up an alternative . . . Immune . . . Hmm.

Perhaps this would suggest a paraphrase from Paul and say somehow that "Emmanuel immunizes us against sin and death and anything else in all creation that tries to separate us from the love of God who is with us in Jesus Christ our Lord!"

The Pastor began to check further, and found more unwitting sorts of witnesses. Guess what? The *"Messiah"* didn't even make it into the Thesaurus! "That Word above all earthly powers" as Luther sang of him couldn't find room among all those other words! No room in the Inn then, and no room in the Thesaurus now!

Ah well, the Pastor thought . . . he made it to Bethlehem . . . and Nazareth . . . and Galilee and Golgotha . . . and was "numbered with the transgressors" . . . and became Christ Jesus our Lord from whose love nothing in all the books or computers in the world can separate us!

In him indeed . . . *"God is with us!"* The "spellcheck" was right. There is no alternative for this!

And so we can sing these days . . .

"Rejoice! Rejoice!
Emmanuel . . . shall come to you.
O captive Israel!"

—from "A View from the Tower," *The Tower Echoes*, First United Methodist and Congregational Church, November 1995.

A Christmas Hymn

Tune: Engelberg 10.10.10 with Alleluias
#810 in United Methodist Hymnal

1. Come, light of light into this heart of night,
Blaze with your glory, banish all our fright,
And grant us wisdom to discern aright,
    Alleluia!

2. Mother of life, bestow on us your Son,
Labor of love, that God's will may be done,
So we, divided now, might all be One.
    Alleluia!

3. Come, boy of joy, and lead us into peace,
Come, fill our hearts, and grant our world release.
From strife and war, and greed and selfishness,
      Alleluia!

4. Shepherds rejoice! And tell it everywhere!
That Christ is born, our sins and griefs to bear!
Let glory fill your hearts instead of fear!
      Alleluia!

5. O righteous ones, long waiting for your God,
Depart in peace, according to his word,
For you have seen the coming of the Lord.
      Alleluia!

6. O world in need, now hear the news again!
How God has come to take away our pain,
And grant us Love to share, and joy to sing:
      Alleluia!

—from Hymns for All Seasons, 1992.

Letter to the Editor
Time Magazine

Surely you jest!

 Your selection of George W. Bush as "Person of the Year" is at best perverse, and at worst malevolent. How about "Bully of the Year"?

 The ancient tradition of the captain going down with the ship was recently confirmed by events in Alaskan waters, but to designate an AWOL pseudo-CEO, ten-gallon-flight-jacket commander-in-chief who with his sorry neo-con crew is hell-bent on sinking the ship of state, taking us down with him; meanwhile egged on by a voyeuristic media and fourth estate who witness his self-destruction while spinning his disasters into "catastrophic success" and bestowing on Dubya such dubious honors as "Person of the Year" is almost too much for my sense of irony to take.

Truly Neil Postman's prophetic word is true; we are a culture "Amusing Ourselves to Death." Have you lost your minds? Or are you contemplating a merger with *The National Inquirer*? I find it hilarious that I got my subscription to *TIME* by way of a contribution to MADD—Mothers Against Drunk Driving.

What was that about power corrupting? Even Journalism?

Mencken . . . thou shoulds't be living at this hour . . . America hath need of thee . . .

Graham Hutchins
Port Angeles, WA

The Ferndale Papers

The Parable of the Unwanted Tree

A few days before Christmas there appeared in front of our church building a Christmas tree, freshly cut, waiting for eager hands to decorate and for eager eyes to enjoy. Someone either donated it to the church or to Project Concern. No one seems to know. Perhaps Project Concern thought it belonged to us. We thought, since our trees were already up, that it belonged to them. I though it would perhaps be given away with a Christmas basket to a needy family, so that they too would enjoy a fresh green tree in the place where they live. But the day after Christmas it was still there! It was never used! Someone cut it down. Someone gave it. No one needed it, or if they did no one received it. It was the unwanted Christmas tree. It simply lay there unclaimed, unused, unwanted, unenjoyed, unshared, or rather, shared but not received.

Is there a parable here? Perhaps I've already stated one, but ever since I saw it lying there so forlorn, on the second day of Christmas, I wondered what sort of meaning we could glean from this tree. I even thought of going down and putting it up two or three days after Christmas and hanging on it a different kind of ornamentation, perhaps something appropriate to its forsakenness. Perhaps pictures of all the unwanted, unused, unreceived meanings, persons, things, given but not received, shared but not rejoiced in, offered but not taken, lovingly bestowed but not gratefully acknowledged.

Is this parable enough? I would invite you to write about it in 150 words or so, what you would do with this tree, how it could be used, what meaning we could gain from this seemingly unimportant, unnoticed, out of the way—yet in front of all—sort of happening. Is it a parable of Christmas? If so, share it with us. Take a piece of paper or even this one and finish the parable, or add to it, or rewrite it, or make up your own, but help us all exhaust the meaning of that tree, the life and death of that tree, and how we cannot let it die in vain but let it contribute to our understanding of the season for which it was sacrificed and unacknowledged. May we hear from you?

—*The United Church Chimes*, United Church, Ferndale, Washington,
January 5, 1981.

A Response to the Parable of the Unwanted Tree

The tree that some people thought was unwanted had already had an important place in an elementary school. You see it had served, with pride and joy, to make many children and adults very happy. Someone thought there was still much value in the green tree, but as so often happens there were those who did not know that it was eager and waiting to be used again. Some people knew and others had been told the story of the Christmas tree but again, as so often happens, they didn't get a full understanding of what happened, and the tree that was willing to serve was not used as fully as it could have been.

[This came in answer to our question in the last Chimes about the unwanted tree.] *United Church Chimes*, Ferndale, WA, February 1981.

A Religion of Choice?

On a Saturday morning a few months ago, Dory and I went to the dress rehearsal concert of the Port Angeles Symphony. We enjoy these concerts and the running commentary by the conductor on the works in progress. We found seats next to a rather sophisticated looking woman with whom we exchanged a few words of greeting. The lights went down and the first number was soon underway. It was a brief work, and at the end I commented that the lights were dimmed more than I had expected and I would find it difficult to read in the dark.

"What are you reading?" the woman asked.

I told her that I am a Pastor and was preparing the next day's sermon, and had brought with me a commentary on the parables to read during the concert.

"What are the parables?" she asked.

Trying to hide my amazement at so basic a question from what seemed such an intelligent lady, I explained a bit about the parables. I mentioned a couple of the more familiar ones in the Gospels, and how they contain the teachings of Jesus about our relationship to God and others.

She seemed rather interested in this and soon launched into a brief discussion of religion while the stage and orchestra were being rearranged for a much larger symphonic piece.

"As for me," she observed, "I believe Buddhism is the best religion for the money."

"Buddhism? . . . Best for the money? Why do you think that?" I asked.

"Because there is compassion in it," she said, "the Buddha knew how to forgive people."

"Are you a Buddhist?" I asked.

"Oh no," she said, "I'm really not religious, but if I were, I think that Buddhism would be the religion to buy into."

The lights went down again as the orchestra resumed the concert. Our conversation had to wait. I was a bit astonished at some of what she was saying to me, so at the next break I ventured to ask, "Don't you agree that there is compassion offered in Christianity?"

She then said several things about how she believed that Christianity just makes people feel guilty and even worse about themselves, and that Jesus foolishly managed to get himself killed at such a young age, etc. . . . I began to wonder what kind of "Christianity" had influenced her. It certainly seemed distorted, legalistic, and judgmental. I found this profoundly sad and reflected much on our conversation during the rest of the concert.

"Here it is," I thought, "right here in Port Angeles . . . Postmodernist, relativistic, incredibly naive multi-cultural consumerism!" "Religion" these days, is something you "buy into" only if you are interested. It is really sort of a "private affair." Something you do solo, rather than in concert. The *truth* of a particular faith is irrelevant. It is of value only if it serves your purpose or your needs. Therefore only a superficial, nodding acquaintance with it is all you require. You can "shop around" the "religious mall" if you like and take your pick. You can have a "religion of choice" . . . like a coffee or a drug. It's your call.

The concert was over. We exchanged a few pleasantries, and then I said, "Remember that at the very heart of Christianity is love, and that means forgiveness, grace, compassion and mercy."

"That may be so," she said, "but if I wanted a religion I'd still buy into Buddhism."

"Then I would suggest you follow the Buddha's *Noble Eightfold Path*," I said, "and when you reach *Nirvana*, where everything matters and nothing matters, you'll find yourself at the foot of the Cross. We'll see you there!"

A few months later, we were in China, at a magnificent Buddhist Temple in Hangzhou. None other than Chou En Lai had spared it from destruction in the Cultural Revolution. Our sad-eyed guide there told us that she herself was not at all "religious" but that her mother was a Buddhist, and that many if not most of the throngs of people buying incense and kneeling at the shrine only choose to do so because it was sort of a "family tradition."

How is it with our faith? . . . Something to think about, isn't it?

—from "A View from the Tower," *The Tower Echoes*, Port Angeles United Methodist and Congregational Church, 1997.

Life Raft

Part I: The Time of Setting Forth

An ancient symbol of the Church is the ship. It was viewed as a vessel, which, like the Ark, carried the people of God through the turbulent waters of chaos safely to their destination. There seems to be plenty of chaos around these days.

Can the Church sail through turbulent waters today? I believe it can and will, but we need some vision of how this is possible.

Have you ever been river rafting? In Hell's Canyon, or on the Salmon River, or elsewhere? Dory and I shared an experience of river rafting a few years ago that brought to mind how appropriate and rich is this ancient symbol of the Church. We embarked on this adventure on the Suiattle River that tumbles out of the North Cascades toward the waters of Puget Sound. In what was seen and said, enjoyed, encountered and done, we discovered a living, moving allegory of the Church that might be appropriate for us to reflect on in these chaotic times.

What did we learn?

First, there was *apprehension*. Misgiving. Do I really want this adventure? *Can I trust this leader and these fellow travelers in this life raft?* As we drove up the river to start on our rafting expedition the water along the way looked rather swift and dangerous. The rapids below appeared very threatening. I'm sure in many people's minds there crossed the thought, "Didn't I have something else to do today?" Is this not how some people feel as they come to the Church for the first time? Or, like the new students coming here to the university who are far from home? Did we feel that way when we faced the possibilities and responsibilities of membership in the Church? Just a little apprehensive?

Second, there was *instruction*. The leader of each nine-person life raft told and demonstrated for us ways of acting and doing that would make the journey possible. He said we needed above all to work together, to follow instructions [even when they didn't seem to make sense], to trust his judgments regarding time and the river, that we might have a safe adventure. After all, he had been down this river before. We had not. We had work to do and we needed to do it consistently together when circumstances called for our concerted action. We would have to paddle in several different ways in order to help him steer us through the rapids. We would welcome the word "relax" and should take it as a command to rest and save our energies for the next task. He gave us instructions on what to do in order to rescue someone who might fall overboard [about this time we *all* decided we needed to be somewhere else!], how to maintain equilibrium, how to hang on in rough water, where to stow the paddles, when to bail . . . etc. We listened very carefully to all this information and took counsel on how to sail together.

After this period of instruction we had sort of a *rite of confirmation* in which we put the raft in the water, climbed aboard, shoved off from the shore and did a few exercises in paddling, turning, and in responding to instructions as given. Then we were off down the river for our great adventure. Feeling confirmed in what we had been taught by our leader we overcame our misgivings and apprehension and set off with an enthusiastic shout!

"Hutch" —a crewman confirmed for an adventure . . .

Next: The River of Commitment

Last time we considered how a river rafting adventure brought to mind the ancient symbol of the Church as a ship sailing on the waters of chaos. We told how we had some *misgivings* about the journey, but took *instruction* on how to proceed and were *confirmed* in that knowledge and set off in *faith.*

Life Raft Part II: A River Called Commitment

As the current carried us off into our stream of adventure and we began to maneuver our raft we soon started to feel the sense of *fellowship* that arises out of shared experience. We got better acquainted with those on board our little ark, and waved and called to other rafts on the river. As we approached the first rapids we heard in the distance the screams of those who had gone on before—which at first sounded to me like the cries of the damned "sailing into the jaws of hell" in Dante's *Inferno.*

Soon we were in the white water ourselves and realized why we were taught that it was in times like this that one must paddle most aggressively. When the river was quiet we rested—when the water ran swiftly we worked like crazy. Is there a parable here? We discovered *we each had work to do, and we really had to work together.* One couldn't paddle just when one felt like it. *Teamwork was of the highest importance,* lest in bumping into each other in our sporadic efforts or failing to do our part we risked losing our way, the raft, the trip and all. To follow the instructions shouted above the roaring water was vital.

We may not have set forth entirely committed to take this journey, but WE SUDDENLY FOUND OURSELVES ON A JOURNEY THAT REQUIRED COMMITMENT. And it was exhilarating! A wild and roaring and risky and fun-filled enterprise together into the unknown challenge of the future!

What an incredible adventure!

Suddenly I found myself bailing—the raft was on the river but the river was increasingly in the raft! It is hard to paddle when you are confronted with a puddle growing at your feet! *Does the chaos of the world sometimes tend to inundate the Church?* Do we need to recognize when the ship is in danger of sinking? Do we sometimes need to "bail" in the life of the Church?

After one wild ride in a stretch of white water Dory exclaimed, "That was so exciting I'd like to do it again!" At which our leader responded, "Would you *all* like to try that one again?" To our collective astonishment we all said, "Yes, yes!" So the next thing we knew we were in a portage and found ourselves stumbling over the rocks along the shore to go back up the river a bit and run it again—carrying the boat that had been carrying us.

Friends, do we sometimes *need to carry the Church which has been carrying us* that we might go on again to new challenges in the faith? Some of the things that were said that day still ring in my ears with implications far beyond a Saturday excursion.

Crewmember to the leader of the crew: "I didn't know when I signed on that I would have to work so hard." —And—"You mean we're *paying* for this? Wait a minute! *You're getting paid* for this and *we're doing all the work!*"

Leader to crew: "One thing we don't stand for is mutiny! No clowning around and pushing each other out. You know I can't do this without you."

Crew to leader: "We sure couldn't do it without you, either!"

The joy of *fellowship: teamwork* that requires *commitment*; the exhilaration of the *challenge; stewardship* born of caring that makes the journey possible; and the *great conversation* along the way!

Such too, is the voyage of Christ's Church!

Paddle on!

"Hutch"—an oarsman, "sailed" by Grace . . .

Next: Time and the River

This concludes a tale of how a river rafting trip became a parable of the Church as a craft of grace on the waters of chaos. Last time we observed how we enjoyed the *fellowship together* of a *challenge that required commitment.* We told of the *caring for each other* and the *teamwork* that made the journey possible, and of the *great conversations* we had as we shared the adventure.

Life Raft Part III: Time and the River

As the currents down the Suiattle River in the North Cascades carried us we found there were times of reflection as well as action. In the quiet stretches of the river along the way there were *stories told by the leader* of other times and rafts on these waters. These were accounts that alerted, inspired, entertained or challenged us to new effort, understanding, appreciation and sharing.

There were tales of strange sights, like that of an old hermit who sometimes appeared on the shore. And there were accounts of the wildlife along the riverbank, that summoned us to watch for a glimpse of rare beauty; such as those of a doe and her fawn coming down to drink, of a bear seeking to feed on the spawning salmon, or of an eagle soaring high above.

We also heard of the mad rush of these waters in early spring, the wild glory of the autumn leaves along the shores and of the solemn beauty of the river in winter.

Sometimes the stories carried a warning—of crews who failed to paddle when they should and foundered on a snag or in the shallows. We were told of Shipwreck Rock and Whitehorse Rapids, and even of the Bellevue High School Logjam that got its name from the crew of a raft that got stranded there.

What a day we had!—As we rode the white water of the river's rapids, rested on its sand bars and beaches, shared our meals, enjoyed each others company, and even grew tired on the journey at the very same time we were incredibly grateful for having made it together. And so it went—it was fun, scary and hilarious all at once! It was a dinghy full of daring-do, of danger and delight! We were in it together and found *we had to believe in the journey; that commitment was no longer an option; participation not just a possibility.*

Is this not the case with the Church as well? We are on a life raft called the Church on a journey of no return and must trust the Leader who knows the River because he's been there before, and need also to learn to trust our fellow crew members who are in the same boat as we are.

Suddenly the Suiattle joined the Sauk and we sailed on the wider stream of the Stillaguamish toward the sea, and were near our journey's end. How filled with a sense of achievement we were! How *grateful for the growth we shared, and the friends we made, and the sights we saw! How glad we were for our time on the river with such a crew!* How worthwhile it was for the little *investment we had all made of planning, time and energy and cost!* How we would be delighted to *bear witness* of the experience to others!

Then our journey with that crew came to an end, on that river, in that place, and at that time.

There are other rivers, other crews, all traveling together toward the sea.

In the Church, God gives us the gift of each other's presence, for a brief sail together to our common destinies in Christ. We can enhance the journey for each other, or we can make shipwreck of the raft of life we are on by how we fail to work together to make it possible. Everyone is needed, everyone is part of the crew, everyone is under the watchful eye and caring of the true Captain of this Ark of Grace that embarks on this grand adventure of faith and time and the river together.

So ends this little account of a most exciting day . . .

Let's sail on!

"Hutch"—a fellow steward on the life raft of Christ.

—from *The Messenger*, Simpson United Methodist Church, Pullman, Washington.

The Palouse Papers

Be Still and Know

During the time of Lent the above-mentioned theme from the 46th Psalm is an excellent rubric for reflection on the meaning of Christ's offering of himself for the world. At present, our world also exhibits abundant evidence of the need for such counsel. We hear of wars and rumors of more wars—of nations and peoples rising up against each other. It was only three-quarters of a century ago that we fought a "War to end all wars." Now we hear of "ethnic cleansing"—of rape as a deliberate strategy of conquest—starvation as another—and terror in our own streets as if we were at war with each other. Have we learned nothing in this bloody century?

Truly . . . as the Psalmist says: "The nations rage . . . and the kingdoms totter." Maybe a frenzied, violent world needs to "Be still . . . and know . . . again . . . that God is God."

The Church has a word to say to all of this. We are not without an answer! We have a word of hope, of comfort, of judgment, of strength to utter to those who despair and are filled "with foreboding at what is coming upon the world." Listen!

"God is our refuge and strength, a very present help in trouble." Therefore, we will not fear though the earth should change, though the mountains shake in the heart of the sea; though its waters roar and foam, though the mountains tremble with its tumult."

Why? Because . . .

"There is a river whose streams make glad the city of God!" And . . . "The Lord of Hosts is with us: the God of Jacob is our refuge."

How well the great reformer Martin Luther knew this. When all the combined forces of Church and Empire and the Bubonic Plague were arrayed against him, he turned to the 46th Psalm . . . was still . . . and knew that God is God . . . and wrote one of the greatest hymns of all time:

"A Mighty Fortress is Our God, a bulwark never failing;
Our helper he amid the flood of mortal ills prevailing . . ."

These are not just words. Mere words cast into the winds of chaos. These are words that are deeds of power. Of strength . . . comfort and hope. Of courage, faith and witness. They are "performative words" as the biblical scholars would say. They get results!

I remember a bitterly cold day near the end of a winter like this. I was called upon to bury a beautiful young girl . . . a senior in high school . . . who had been killed in an automobile accident. At the cemetery I not only faced a whole community, but felt confronted with literally waves of grief . . . a wild and restless sea of sorrow and chaos. Suddenly the words of this Psalm came to me and I said,

"Be still!—And know that God . . . is God!

I was and am still astonished at the great calm that came upon that scene. The word of God is mighty . . . mighty indeed!

We are far too timid as the Church sometimes. The word entrusted to us is "powerful in its effect, even to the pulling down of strongholds and proud imaginations!"

"Come, behold the works of the Lord!
Who has wrought desolations in the earth;
who makes wars cease to the ends of the earth,
breaks the bow . . . shatters the spear, and burns the chariots with fire!

"Be still! And know that God . . . is God!"

—from The Messenger, Simpson United Methodist Church, Pullman,
Washington 1989.

The Palouse Papers

The Moment of the Hollyhocks

What? What is that? That color? That light? That golden radiance? Those giant blossoms ablaze with light?

It is warm here . . . I feel the rough texture of the leaves . . . but most of all . . . the Light! The blazing red and orange and golden glory of it all! What a discovery! What a world! May it never end! May I delight in it forever!

Such is an articulation of my memory of an intense experience . . . one of the awakening moments of my total awareness. It was very simple . . . and yet . . . utterly profound. It is with me still, as an unforgettable numinous moment of my early childhood. I call it the "moment of the hollyhocks."

They grew in our yard in Boulder, Colorado, where we lived at that time, and I had seen them many times I'm sure . . . but in that moment . . . the one of which I write . . . I *discovered* them . . . and also in that moment something discovered me . . . or awoke within me.

It was probably my first awareness of the numinous reality of the world. I was immersed in the vivid luminosity of what to a small child were the giant blossoms of the hollyhock radiant in the sunlight. They

92

were over me, around me, beside me, beneath me . . . and most of all *awake within me.*

I was astonished . . . and in ecstasy . . . and wondered at the intense beauty of it all . . . the warmth . . . the light . . . the color . . . the radiance. Both the awakened awareness of the world and the equally profound *awareness of that awakening.*

The hollyhock ever since has been one of my favorite flowers, even at times when I haven't seen one for years; perhaps because I can see them in my memory at any moment of recall, restoring to me the vivid awareness of the wonderful astonishment they gave to me.

Have you had such moments? Sudden encounters with the wonder of life that brings fresh insight into the heart of things? It can happen anywhere. Like at the sacrament of the Lord's Table where the ordinary food that sustains us can suddenly convey the very wonder of God. Or think of Jacob . . . not a very likable sort of man . . . running from his family whom he has alienated. He sleeps in the wilderness with a rock for a pillow . . . has incredible dreams . . . and wakes up to the wonder of the world and the presence of God. His exclamation might be ours as well. . . . "Truly, the Lord was in this place and I did not know it!" Such, I think, was that "moment of the hollyhocks" to me.

Reflect on *your* experience and life and think about how the ordinary can convey the luminous reality of God. As we gather this Sunday at the Table of the Lord with Christians around the world let us be open to that moment that—we might discover afresh the incredible wonder and presence of God.

—from *The Messenger,* Simpson United Methodist Church, Pullman, Washington, September 1989.

Some Other Paper Trails . . .

On this, the 2nd Anniversary of the current Iraq war . . . We need to reflect on what is happening . . . to us . . . as well as to the world . . . Ponder the statements below . . .

"In War, truth is the first casualty."
—Aeschylus, Greek Tragic Dramatist, 525-426 B.C.

"Practically the whole of the Hellenic world was convulsed, with the rival parties in every state . . . democratic leaders trying to bring in the Athenians, and oligarchs trying to bring in the Spartans . . .

To fit in with the change of events, words, too, had to change their usual meanings. What used to be described as a thoughtless act of aggression was now regarded as the courage one would expect to find in a party member, to think of the future and wait was merely another way of saying one was a coward; any idea if moderation was just an attempt to disguise one's unmanly character; ability to understand a question from all sides meant that one was totally unfitted for action.

Fanatical enthusiasm was the mark of a real man, and to plot against an enemy behind his back was perfectly legitimate self-defense. Anyone who held violent opinions could always be trusted, and anyone who objected to them became a suspect. . . . As a result . . . there was a general deterioration of character throughout the Greek world. The plain way of looking at things, which is so much the mark of a noble nature, was regarded as a ridiculous quality and soon ceased to exist. Society became divided into camps in which no man trusted his fellow."

—Thucydides, History of the Peloponnesian War, ca. 400 B.C.

. . . of whom it has been said: "His determination to look reality in the face was unswerving, even to the point of showing how war—this war and all wars—causes the degeneration of society."

—Thomas Cahill, Sailing the Wine Dark Sea—Why the Greeks Matter

"There is no morality in war. Morality is the privilege of those judging from the distance. War is only death and destruction, regardless of which scripture is quoted. War is the tool of small-minded scoundrels who worship the death of others on the altar of their greed. War is the cemetery of futures promised. War is eternity jammed into frantic minutes that will fill a lifetime with dreams and nightmares."

—The conclusion to an October 1, 2004 article by John Cory, a wounded and decorated Vietnam War veteran.

O God of earth and altar, Bow down and hear our cry; Our earthly rulers falter, Our people drift and die; The walls of gold entomb us, The swords of scorn divide; Take not Thy thunder from us, But take away our pride.

From all that terror teaches, From lies of tongue and pen; From all the easy speeches, That comfort cruel men; From sale and profanation Of honor and the sword; From sleep and from damnation, Deliver us, good Lord!

Tie in a living tether The prince and priest and thrall; Bind all our lives together, Smite us and save us all; In ire and exultation, Aflame with faith, and free, Lift up a living nation, A single sword to Thee.

—G.K. Chesterton, 1874-1936

Those who refuse to learn from history are destined to repeat its mistakes.

—George Santayana, 1863-1952

The Monitor Papers

Real Presence

Behind
This bread and wine
    Are eyes
That see through me
And search the secret places
    Of my heart,
That move me to awareness
Of his love and care,
And summon forth the shame
He bids depart.

Can He,
Who in that Upper Room
So long ago,
Named bread his flesh
    and wine his life,
Can He,

Who drank to each last drop
Our cup of woe,
Be with us now?
To meet with us
        in bread and blood?
Or is it wine and flesh?
These symbols merge!
He willed it so!
That we,
As that small band
Might share it new,
That Supper Last
        Yet First . . .
And see these eyes
That love us, too.

He is not there, but here!
Or, rather say,
That here . . . is there!
        No matter!
This banquet is forever!
Because the Host . . .
Betrayed . . . denied, deserted . . .
Delivered to the dead!
Came back again!
        Alive! Anew!
And meets with us
In bread and wine . . . Not seen . . .
And yet!
        "My Lord!" . . . "My God!"
Not lost to view.

—from *A Word in Season*, Graham Hutchins, 1998, 1971.

A Hymn of Pentecost

Tune: Sine Nomine 10.10.10. with Alleluias
#166 The United Methodist Hymnal

1. Creator Spirit, calling worlds to be,
Renew our earth again and set us free
From strife and hatred to true liberty:
    Alleluia! Alleluia!

2. Redeeming Spirit, come and be our guest,
For night comes on and we must seek our rest,
As we break bread, now, let our souls be blest:
    Alleluia! Alleluia!

3. Come Holy Spirit, spirit of the Son,
Sent from the Father, making all things One,
Come, fill your Church, and make each heart your home,
    Alleluia! Alleluia!

4. Spirit of God, our Source and Grace and Power,
Descend once more; upon this place and hour,
Granting again, your gifts and fruit and fire!
    Alleluia! Alleluia!

5. Spirit of Love, of Righteousness and Peace,
Call us anew, to witness to your grace,
That all the world at last may see Christ's face:
    Alleluia! Alleluia!

—from *Hymns for All Seasons*, 1992.

The Town That Isn't There . . .

Have you ever noticed when you were driving through a town not too many miles from here that you never see anyone—"there"? It is an impressive looking town! The houses are well kept, the lawns all mowed, the flower beds neat . . . all seems to be in good order . . . but there is no one to be seen anywhere! Once, while driving by, my wife saw through a lighted window a man sitting in a rocking chair, but we are wondering now if it really was a man or just a mannequin.

It is an historical old town for these parts, and is on the register. A sign at the end of the street leading down to the empty waterfront reads: "Founded in 1853." Maybe those who founded it back then all died of some mysterious plague and left the place to a strange guild of caretakers who emerge from somewhere in the middle of the night to cut the grass and turn out the lights. We played a sort of game to that effect recently, while passing through with our grandchildren, offering a prize to the first one who managed to see someone. None of us did, so none of us won!

There are a few cars . . . parked here and there . . . but no one on the streets . . . no children at play, no people at all . . . not even any dogs or cats! Who is it that turns on and off those sprinklers on the lawns? The place looks deserted. There is even a lovely little church, but no one is ever seen entering or leaving. [I'm tempted to send someone by on a Sunday morning to see if anyone shows up for worship.] We stopped at the little museum in the town and a notice read . . . "Closed for filming" . . . but no one was taking pictures! Except us! Maybe the whole town is a museum, or a cemetery with streetlights, with houses for tombstones? The last time passing through we saw a sign that said . . . *GARAGE SALE* . . . and if we hadn't been in a rush to get somewhere else we would have followed the directions just to see if anyone was buying or selling. Even when the local mill was running we never saw anyone coming or going to or from work. Maybe they all worked the "graveyard" shift then, and now commute to employment in more urban centers? Perhaps they are all out shopping . . . elsewhere! Might they go to church in another place? The only people we ever see are travelers—who, like us, are going to and from the ferry. A ghostly place! Strange!

Is there a parable here? Someone once said the Church is a hospital for sinners, not a museum for saints. We find a church building in that town, and a museum, but no hospital. We find no saints *or* sinners in that church, museum or town!—*We don't find anyone!*

Do we have sinners and saints in our church and town? Do others see *us* as caretakers of a museum . . . or as the saints of God? *Or do they just not see us at all?* Maybe we aren't alive enough or "present" enough to be noticed. Maybe not radical enough to make people passing by stop and find out what's going on! Perhaps we should have a garage sale!

But this certainly isn't true of our church! We have a lot going on all the time! And last week we were really a beehive of activity! The Vacation Bible School was amazing! No deserted town this! Rather a thriving marketplace in the "wilderness" and a people out to "build a holy place" and live for God! A lot of people noticed what was going on! I was asked if we were having a "revival" because of the big tent outside! I should have said, "Yes . . . we're living who we were 3,400 years ago under Moses, who is reviving us."

The Church is always dying and being reborn. Always being torn down and rebuilding. We are too haunted by the saints to be like a "ghost town!" Too enlivened by the "Holy Ghost" to be a "dead church"! We preach an Empty Tomb that will fill the Church and the world with good news again and again! We are not like a "town that isn't there," but are those who set out to "build a holy place" on our way to the City of God!

Onward . . . Toward the Promises!

—from "A View from the Tower," First United Methodist and Congregational Church, Port Angeles, Washington, August 14, 1997.

The Feast of Fools

"Life is just too important to be taken seriously."

This word from Oscar Wilde is one of my favorite quotes. It seems to express a profound truth about how to maintain a certain kind of balance in life that is neither shallow carelessness nor gloomy seriousness. So often we seem to be so concerned about life that we can kill our enjoyment of it. Or, we trivialize it to the point of not seeing how important it truly is. We are either afraid to have fun, or afraid to have anything else. We need to learn to laugh at ourselves. And we need to learn to truly value the importance of things. Life is not a game of Trivial Pursuit. But it is full of fun.

There is an often forgotten festival in the Christian calendar that expresses this same wisdom. It is called the *Feast of Fools*, and it often took place on *Shrove Tuesday,* just before the beginning of *Lent,* the most somber and serious season of the year.

Lent was a solemn fast . . . when the faithful gave up things in a spiritual discipline that weighed the importance of life in the light of Christ's awesome gift of love even to his death on the Cross for us. Some of the things often given up for *Lent* were the foods that were most enjoyable and fattening and sinfully delicious. So before the fast began there was a quick feast in which these things were consumed in a final last hurrah before the rigors of Lenten observance. This is why *Shrove Tuesday* got nicknamed "*Fat Tuesday*" and why the *Feast of Fools* was appropriate as a way to poke fun at the seriousness of life without doing so during *Lent.* In short, it was a kind of late winter *Halloween,* when everyone could enjoy a time of feasting and frivolity. It was an opportunity for wearing costumes and pretending you are someone else. Peasants could be bishops for a day. Bishops could be peasants. Paupers reigned as king for a day. Kings could pretend to be knaves with no responsibility for the heavy obligations of governance. Everybody could poke fun at everybody else for a short time and then go back to the important things refreshed. So as *Lent* prepared the people for the joy of *Easter, Fat Tuesday* prepared them for the solemnity of *Lent*. On *Shrove Tuesday* they had a carnival around the joys of life. The next day, *Ash Wednesday* began *Lent* and reminded them they are "of the dust, and to dust they shall return."

T.S. Eliot once observed that "humankind cannot bear too much reality." We seem to need the *rhythm* of life to keep it balanced and going. "Life is just too important to be taken seriously." All the time anyway! Fasting has its needed place. May we also delight in the feasting and the foolishness of life!

Are you enjoying the foolish feast of life?

—from *The Messenger*, Simpson United Methodist Church, Pullman, Washington, 1988.

The Palouse Papers

Where Are Wise Men?

We have just celebrated the Feast of the Epiphany with the observance of the coming of the Wise Men to seek out the child Jesus—born to be the "King of the Jews." The Wise Men offered up their costly treasure in homage to this Child. They are symbolic of the wisdom and power of the nations acknowledging that the one born King of the Jews is Lord and Savior of the world.

One of the titles of our Lord is "The Prince of Peace." Is this just pious rhetoric, or does it mean what it says?

We say that Jesus is the "Way." Is this just "religious language?" Or does it have something to do with how we make our way through life? If Jesus is the "Way" and the "Prince of Peace" and this has something to do with the world then the wise of every age will seek to follow the Child who will lead them into the "peaceable kingdom." Wise Men and Women recognize that this Child can lead us into the ways of Peace. *With Jesus, Peace is the Way as well as the Goal.*

The world refuses to learn this truth. Nearly 2,000 years of

Christian history demonstrate this refusal. And 10,000 years of human history demonstrate that the result of war is not peace but conquest; not life, but death; not a renewed but a devastated earth and a violated humanity.

There are very few wars in history that can be justified in terms of the Doctrine of the "Just War" promulgated by the Church beginning with St. Augustine in the 4th Century. The one we are at great risk in being involved in is not. Nor was "Operation 'Just Cause' " in Panama, in spite of the fact that it's title was stolen from the "Just War" doctrine of the Roman Catholic Church.

One of the stipulations of the "Just War" doctrine is that the cause for going to war must be a just one. Another is that noncombatants not be killed. To kill about 3,000 people to capture a drug lord like Manuel Noriega, who for years was on our payroll, is hardly a "just cause." Nor, in the Middle East, is killing our young adult men and women and thousands of our newfound "enemies"—to say nothing of the innocent civilians caught in this mess—a "just war." Nor is going to war for "jobs" or "oil" or our right to be homeless or in debt in the "American Way."

I often think the real prophets of our society are the cartoonists. A cartoon handed to me by one of our members asks . . . "Where are the Wise Men?" This cartoon, by Shoe . . . asserts that this Christmas our troops in the Middle East could really use something that we haven't seen in those parts for quite some time . . . Wise Men . . . and shows a tank ready for some other act of war.

We all want "peace." Is there a wise way to achieve it? We can differ on that. But what we do need to know—remember and share—is the story of our faith and the implications of it for our world. Where *are* the Wise Men? Maybe the New Testament can tell us more: Go and read, reflect on, and inwardly digest . . . I Corinthians 1:20-31.

Vigil of Prayer for Peace

As we are all aware, events in the Middle East seem to be headed for a major conflict unless the problem is resolved diplomatically. As Christians and as citizens we are all concerned; therefore, the Council on Ministries is calling you to participate in a vigil of prayer for peace here at Simpson United Methodist Church on January 13th beginning at 8:00 P.M.

The churches in the Pullman Inter-Church Council plan to join us in this vigil. We will begin with a brief service at 8:00 P.M. at which members of other congregations and individuals in the community are invited for corporate worship and prayer. Following that persons may stay or return for a period *of* time of individual prayer and meditation throughout the night.

You may sign up for a half-hour (or more) period of time between 8:30 P.M. on January 13th and 8:00 A.M. on January 14th. The sign up sheet will be on a board in the narthex.

—from The Messenger, Simpson United Methodist Church, Pullman,
Washington, January 10, 1991.

The Palouse Papers

To Insure Payment?

It was a good dinner. We enjoyed it. We were well fed and well served. As we gathered ourselves together to leave we went through a little ritual of social custom:

"How much shall we give the waitress?"

"Let's see . . . the customary amount is fifteen percent . . . right?"

"Right."

So we each left about fifteen percent of what our meals cost. We were all busy people and eat out several times a week. And we usually feel obligated to tip those who serve us and are aware that the expected tip in our culture is approximately fifteen percent.

Do we leave a tip when the food is lousy and the service poor? Maybe not as much . . . maybe only ten percent . . . or even five percent. But then things go through our heads like . . . "He's not the cook, and can't help it if the food is bad." Or . . . "This is a student working her way through college . . . give her a break . . . even if she was too busy to get me more coffee . . . etc."

Do thoughts like these ever go through *your* head?

It was a great service. We enjoyed it. The choir sang like they were at the very gates of heaven. The lay reader did well. The sermon wasn't too bad either. And that wonderful prelude! And the sun falling on the Cross on the chancel wall. Good hymns today! Did you see those kids' faces during the children's talk? And when we prayed for those who were lonely and homeless I felt a new sense of how we need to reach out to others. How blessed we are to be able to gather each week and greet each other in the fellowship of the Church. And when we said the benediction—"The Lord bless you and keep you"—I knew again that truly—God *is* good! It was a good service! Near the end . . . as the offering was taken I put in my usual . . .

"A tithe?"

"Oh no!—but I give well . . . we've a lot of bills you know. Besides, how do you figure what a tithe is? Is it ten percent of your *gross* income—or of your *net* income? And we give to other causes as well. It was a great service though . . . Wish I could give more . . . We went to dinner afterwards . . . It was good dinner . . . We enjoyed it. We were well fed and well served. As we gathered ourselves together to leave we went through a little ritual of social custom . . . How much shall we give the . . . ?"

Wait a minute! I'm tithing the waitress and tipping God!

What is going on here? I've formed some very interesting habits indeed! I keep giving the same tip I always have—"<u>T</u>o <u>I</u>nsure <u>P</u>ayment"—as they say—and I've given the same amount at church for years. *Could it really be that I'm tithing the waitress and tipping God?* Of course, fifteen percent of a lunch bill is certainly a lot less than even one percent of my income . . . which is what I usually give at church. Or is it? If I eat out five times a week on my busy schedule and tip fifteen percent of it—what would it amount to? Would it be more than I give to God once a week?

Maybe I'm giving a tithe of a tithe to God—and a tithe and a half to the waitress! Something to think about!! . . . Meanwhile . . . it was a great service this morning and a wonderful dinner afterwards! God has indeed blessed us!

Christ gives of himself every day to feed us in loving service all our days. "Let's see . . . what shall *we* give?" Do thoughts like this ever go through *your* head?

—from *The Messenger,* Simpson United Methodist Church, September 1989.

"Happy" and Heraclitus*

I was reading about Heraclitus
        when it must have happened.
Our little dog and a car couldn't
        occupy the same place
        in the great flux of the world.

His form was changed—
        the car probably just
        got bloodied up a bit,
        as did my arm,
with his warm, moist, life.

Who did it? Does it even matter?
        These things happen.
But a happy dog with a happy soul,
        Is now just a happy soul.
Traveling on—somewhere—in his
        love of wandering.

The river of life runs down our faces . . .
        It didn't hold him long.
        The doggone little dog
            is gone!
        Leaving fire in our souls.

Happy travels! "Happy"!

*Heraclitus—a pre-Socratic philosopher who sought to explain the process of change or
"flux" in the world. He contended you "cannot step into the same river twice," because
of the flux in the cosmos. Rivers and souls, indeed, all things are in constant change and
yet remain the same. This unity in diversity he argued can be accounted for by the transforming element of fire. This "ever-living Fire" constantly changes everything fed into it
. . . into something else. Fire condensed becomes "the moist" and this becomes water,
which congealed becomes earth. On the "upward path" this process is reversed. In this
constant change of form in the process of the world is the universal law or "reason" of
the Universe.

You made us happy too.

—from A Word in Season

The Seattle Papers

What? *Me* Witness?

"... and you will be my witnesses to the ends of the earth."

—Acts 1:8.

We were having lunch one day at the Wesley House dining room. At the table with us was a soldier, who used to drop by on some of his days off to be again in a college environment. After graduating from the University of Wisconsin he had joined the Army and was now stationed at Fort Lewis. On this day he happened to mention that he was being transferred to Fort Richardson in Alaska. I told him I had been to Alaska on a Student Work Camp and knew of a good Young Adult group in a church in Anchorage that he might like to check out. Our conversation ended and I never saw him again.

Some three or four years later I was in Lawrence, Kansas, at the Quadrennial Methodist Student Movement Conference at the University of Kansas, during the Christmas break. For several days at that busy conference I kept getting messages that a student from the University of California was looking for me. "But I don't know anyone from the University of California," I replied each time with some puzzlement.

Then one night when I was in bed, and it was after midnight, the door to my dorm room opened and I saw a head silhouetted against the light of the hallway and a voice said:

"Graham Hutchins?"

"Yes," I said.

"I've been looking for you," the voice said.

"Are you from the University of California?" I asked.

"I am," he said, "and I've been looking for you for days."

"How is it you know me," I said. "And who are you, anyway?"

"My name is Al de S . . . . . ," he replied, "and a few years ago when I was in the Army, I came through the Wesley Foundation at the University of Washington in Seattle and you told me to go to a young adult group at a church in Anchorage. Well, I went to that church as you directed, and I became a Christian, and I just wanted to find you and thank you."

He told me he was now in Graduate School at Berkeley studying nuclear physics, but was forever grateful that I had by a word led him to where he had opportunity to become a Christian. "Thank you again," he said, and the door closed . . . and he was gone, and I was filled with wonder for awhile . . . and then fell into an amazed and grateful sleep.

If you ever doubt the effectiveness of your "witness" to anyone, I hope you will remember this story of how I was a witness for Christ without even hardly thinking about it. I just said a word to a stranger at a lunch table. Yet It changed his life! Never underestimate the influence of *your* word and witness!

You, too—might say a word that will change a life!

The Palouse Papers

"Bonehead" Church History!!! ?

I have received a number of responses to this quiz on Church History, requesting the "answers!" People from Port Angeles to Jakarta are wanting me to supply these. Since I first sent this out in 1990 and lost the "answer sheet" I had to do a bit more research for some of the questions to supply it! Thank God for Google! I realize that I share their frustration when from time to time I try to answer a quiz in the paper and don't get the answers the "next day" . . .

What does the United Methodist Publishing House have to do with a

monastery in England where you could stay as a guest and have your horse shod overnight?

They share the name . . . Abingdon. Abingdon on Thames is Britain's "oldest town." The ancient Abingdon Abbey was a wealthy monastery that got trashed by King Henry VIII in his "dissolution of the monasteries" in the 16th century. At that time it was the 6th wealthiest monastery in England. Probably because it was such a good "bed and breakfast" place? Abingdon on Thames still has a thriving "Monday market." Why the United Methodist publishing enterprise stole the name I haven't yet discovered!

Who was the patron saint of people with toothaches? And why?

There are at least seven. Must have been lots of aching teeth in the world! The most famous is Apollonia; or Appoline . . . virgin, deaconess, martyr. Her teeth were broken with pincers and she was given the choice between renouncing Christ and being burned alive. She lept into the fire herself. She died in 249, at Alexandria. She is the patron saint of dentists and those with toothache. She is pictured as an aged deaconess holding pincers and a tooth . . . or a tooth and a palm branch.

What great Christian leader expected to see his dog in heaven?

Can't remember where I read this! Might be Martin Luther. Sounds like him!

What passionate romance in Church history rivals that of Romeo and Juliet in literature? Did Shakespeare steal the story from us?

Abelard and Heloise—in 12th-century Paris . . . the famous philosopher Abelard takes the brilliant and lovely niece of a canon of Notre Dame as a student. They fall in love and what follows is a tragic and beautiful story much like *Romeo and Juliet*. Their love and ideas are expressed in a lively correspondence before they met and after they are separated. They fell passionately in love, finally had a child, were secretly married, and then forcefully separated. . . . Abelard then becomes a monk and Heloise a nun . . . they still wrote each other . . . and met again, later in life . . . all the passion and love and intrigue is an amazing story. Now made into a musical.

Who was the Mayor who went from Baptism to Bishop in less than a week?

Ambrose of Milan . . . elected bishop by acclamation when he went into the cathedral . . . it moved him to conversion and then baptism. He became one of the great preachers, bishops, and hymn writers of the church. Augustine was moved by his preaching toward his own conversion. Ambrose bravely barred the emperor from the church after a massacre of a village.

Matthew, Mark. Luke and John are known as the four Evangelists. Who is the known as the fifth? Why? What did he write?

Johann Sebastian Bach . . . whose music for the church . . . written . . . *Soli Deo Gloria* . . . [to the glory of God] is worthy of a place in the canon of scripture. Actually, most of it is scripture, set to glorious music.

Did you know that the beloved Pope John the 23rd was really John 23 the second? Who was the first?

Pope John the 23rd the First. Seven renegade cardinals rebelled against Pope Gregory XII and called a council at Pisa and elected their own pope . . . now called "anti-popes." This was in 1409. Their new "Pope" lasted a year, and was replaced by John XXIII in 1410-1415. He was charged with all kinds of things . . . mostly trumped up . . . and there were no more Pope Johns for centuries. The twentieth-century Pope John XXIII changed all that by taking the title and giving it honor and now is known as the "Blessed Pope John XXIII."

What great church leader was called to engage in a Diet of Worms?

This is a play on words. Luther was called to the "Diet" . . . [a convocation] of the Church at the city of Worms . . . pronounced . . . in German . . . *Vorms* . . . to be confronted with his protestant heresies. It was here he contended that he stood on scripture alone . . . and said . . . "Here I stand, I can do no other . . . so help me God."

Name five great Christian works written in jail.

About half the New Testament: the "Captivity Epistles: *Philippians, Colossians, Philemon* and *Ephesians*; and the *Book of Revelation*. Also, works like *Pilgrim's Progress* by John Bunyan, *Letters and Papers from Prison*, by Dietrich Bonhoeffer, etc.

Sounds like "Trivial Pursuit"? Church History can be interesting and fun. Care for some different kinds of questions? Church History can be a "significant pursuit," very important for our lives and faith and understanding. Try these:

Do you call yourself a Protestant? What does that mean? A "non-Catholic"?
If that is all you mean, you need to do some study!

Is the Church the great enemy of science? Or the great sponsor of science?
Claims are made for both charges. The church reprimanded Galileo for example . . . but it encouraged Copernicus. Biblical faith is one of the presuppositions, or foundation assumptions . . . i.e., articles of faith on which modern science is built and proceeds . . . as in the doctrine of creation demonstrating divine order in the world. See, for example, a classic in the philosophy of science . . . Alfred North Whitehead, *Science and the Modern World*. The current so-called clash between the Bible and science is mostly a caricature of both pitted against each other.

How is prejudice related to Church History? Or, conversely, to an ignorance of Church History?
Compare the daily news with some Church history. Most of the prejudice we witness is old stuff, either in ancient heresies reborn or some of the arguments against them. Prejudice can have a "liberal" bias . . . a "conservative" bias or even a "neutral" "fair and balanced" bias. Some disputes get settled . . . and then forgotten . . . and are reborn as modern prejudice. Like some of the modern disputes about science, evolution, the Bible, etc. . . . . aspersions and accusations are cast about and animosity grows and nobody studies or seeks to resolve disputes in a thoughtful careful way.

Has anyone ever believed the way I do? If so, who? And why?
Very likely! Only you can find out.

Was Jesus a Christian?
No . . . he was a Jew . . . who he was and what he did is the

foundation of Christianity . . . this would be like saying "were the Pilgrim fathers Americans?"

What do alarm clocks have to do with Church History?
Monks developed the alarm clock to remind them when to say their prayers . . . As in the canonical hours . . .

Come! . . . let us pursue trivia . . . and significance . . . together.

"Hutch" Your Pastor, from *The Messenger*, Simpson United Methodist Church, Pullman, Washington, January 1990.

The Ferndale Papers

Etched Windows

On Pentecost Sunday, May 30, we dedicated the windows in the entryway of our church. Purchased with memorial funds and the etching "sand blasted" by one of our members, Winfred "Buster" Atkinson, the windows are designed to be a fitting expression of what at our best we are called to be as The United Church. What does this mean?

The United Church of Ferndale was and is an ecumenical adventure. Two small churches of different tradition and history decided they could work and grow together because they both belonged to a wider vision of the CHURCH. As an ecumenical enterprise it is an adventure in reconciliation. People of different persuasion had confidence that they could learn to live together in harmony and peace, that the beauty and richness of diversity is far greater than the scandal and pain of division. The symbols etched on these new windows explore the biblical basis of this vision. These are multiple symbols that mean something in themselves but when taken together imply something even greater, just as the biblical story unfolds with all of its diversity and meaning to reveal an even greater unity and richness in its totality.

The *Lion*, the "King of the Beasts," is the symbol of strength. In the Bible we find the lion is the symbol of Judah, and then of the Judean King David, who becomes the type of the Messiah. Jesus is born of the house of David and becomes the fulfillment of that messianic hope, the Lord's anointed, the Christ. He is the messianic king, the Lion of Judah. Because we belong to Jesus we are *a royal people* with a faith that overcomes the world in the strength of the Lord.

The *Lamb,* is the symbol of sacrifice, of the offering of life for the sake of the community. This symbol first appears in the Bible in the book of Genesis when Abraham offers his son, Isaac, and God spares him, announcing that God himself would provide a lamb for the offering. The lamb reappears throughout the Old Testament as the symbol of innocence, gentleness, and divine sacrifice for the sins of the people. As the Passover Lamb it symbolizes the blood shed in the deliverance of God's people from slavery to freedom, bondage to liberty, death to life. The New Testament sees in Jesus Christ the Lamb of God who is offered and offers himself, as the one perfect and sufficient sacrifice for the sins of the whole world. He gives himself over to death that we might have forgiveness and life. Because we belong to Jesus we are *a priestly-servant people,* and share his grace and life with the world.

The *Wheat,* is the symbol of growth, of nourishment, of bread, of life shared in community. Jesus said, "Except a grain of wheat fall into the ground and die, it abides alone, but if it dies to itself it bears much fruit." A grain of wheat brings out of itself a whole sheaf of wheat. We take wheat to grind it to make bread. Bread nourishes our bodies and our life. The Passover bread becomes the body of Christ, broken for us, and put to death for us, that we might have life together and that abundant.

The cluster of *Grapes* is a symbol of the people of God. Israel was the vineyard of the Lord called to bear fruit for God. As the wheat is ground, so the grapes are crushed to make wine, the symbol of life and spirit and joy. Jesus is the true vine and we are the branches. As we abide in Him, we bear much fruit. His life was crushed and poured out for us. As often as we drink the cup of his forgiveness, we show forth his sacrifice and gain strength and life to be his joyful people in the world.

These symbols taken together mean even something more. The Lion of Judah became the Lamb of God who takes away the sin of the world. The strength made perfect in weakness is the source of our reconciliation, forgiveness and peace. Forgiveness and reconciliation lead to the "peaceable kingdom," where the lion shall lie down with the lamb and all shall be secure. The wheat and the grapes become the bread and wine of the sacrament that announces to us the forgiveness and grace of God, the food and drink of His people who become one body in Christ, sharing in the new life of God's Kingdom.

In their totality these symbols proclaim even more for the life of the church. The strength of love that offers itself for others creates a growing community of life together, of sharing and service and joy and peace in the Lord. We here, in this place, can be and are that growing, rejoicing community of this new life together—united in the peace of the Lord.

—from *The Chimes*, Ferndale United Church, Ferndale, Washington, June 28, 1982.

The Jakarta Journal

Leprosy—Luxury—Need

He stands amid the traffic every day, his hands out with a hat for coins given to him by the passing motorists. He makes his living this way . . . and those in the cars that pass understand that this is the only income he has. You can see that his hands and body are deformed. He is a leper. Leprosy is now curable—but for this man, and others here, it came too late. He reminds one, amid the din of this horrendous traffic, that the ancient disease we thought was just in Bible stories, is yet a reality for many people in the world, and also in this city of more than 15 million souls. It was a strange encounter on the very day we had read in church the Advent lesson about how the lepers will be cleansed and the poor have the good news preached to them through the new thing God would do for the world in his love.

We entered the mall through its grand front entrance and found ourselves confronted by a great central atrium. To the right of the center of this we saw a fully lighted Christmas tree at least five storeys high . . .

near its base was a huge orchid colored sleigh on which sat a Santa receiving children with their wishes for the holiday. As we rode up the escalator we noticed on a stage near the tree an ensemble of young men in tuxedos who began to sing:

Go Tell it On the Mountain . . . Over the hills and everywhere . . . Go
    tell it on the Mountain . . . That Jesus Christ is Born.

Nearing the height level with the top of the giant Xmas tree we noticed an ice rink and on the next landing a food court boasting any fast food one could want. There are also restaurants on various floors, and furniture stores that boast the finest money can buy, a Warner Bros. Studio Store, art galleries, and fashion boutiques with the latest in European or American clothing from the most famous designers in the world. We got some lunch . . . Dory, a Thai salad, and Graham, a chicken croissant sandwich . . . in a small "French" café off the balcony of the top landing. Huge glass elevators meanwhile carried people up and down to where they could shop in air-conditioned luxury. Descending to the main floor to meet met our driver, Paul, we paused on the third landing to note that the musical group below were now singing about a Christmas that few in this huge mall complex would ever remember, and most could hardly imagine:

. . . where the tree tops glisten, and children listen, to hear sleigh bells
    in the snow.

We marveled at the incredible incongruity of it all! On the bottom floor is a supermarket with marble floors and boasting displays that would make envious any grocer in the world. After shopping at this outlet of a well-known local chain, we proceeded to the parking garage on the same level and noted that it had an attractively designed floor of inlaid ceramic tiles that would grace any fine home with style.

This was the *Mal Taman Anggrek* . . . or "Orchid Mall." It is in Jakarta, Indonesia, a developing country . . . as they say . . . in the tropics . . . south of the Equator . . . and in a nation with the highest population of Muslims in the world.

Further on, in the rush of traffic, was a small child, less than five years old who holds out his hands for coins, along with his older brothers

and a sister as they seek to find a way to live in this city. The little child
seems right at home among the endless cars and countless motorcycles
that weave in and out around him. At home, in America, there would be
instant panic to see a child that age so close to bumper-to-bumper rush
hour lines of cars as far as the eye can see. He has a warm smile on his
face, and says *terima kasih*—"thank you" . . . to all who hand him coins
or bills from the passing cars. It is an incredible sight. The traffic flows
on . . . night and day . . . like a great river with multiple tributaries as
people make way for each other in order to ride the flow to where they
need to go. And the Child is there . . . With his smile and open hand . . .
and word of thanks . . . and he brings to mind as we encounter him another word from long ago . . . that . . . *inasmuch as we give unto the least
of these . . . we give to Him . . .*

—from *The Jakarta Journal,* 1999-2000.

The Palouse Papers

The Colors of Our Patriotism

Editor, *The Daily News/Idahonian*   February 24, 1991

The great flap in this community and country regarding *yellow ribbons,* and who should or should not wear them, what they really mean,
and why, is as about as relevant to the crisis that has overtaken this nation
as a similar discussion in Russia early in this bloodstained century. The
Russian Orthodox Church was seriously debating the use of *yellow* in liturgical vestments when the Bolshevik Revolution drowned their discussions in a sea of violence. Color it Red.

When the present conflict in the Persian Gulf comes to its end, we
will still have a lot more important questions to deal with than the colors
of our patriotism. Are all the ribbons and flags we see really symbols of a
freedom that is vanishing and a republic that is perishing under the
weight of its own arrogance? The question may not just be, "Who will rebuild Kuwait and Iraq," but, as it already loomed before the conflict

began, "Who will rebuild America?" Does our vaunted "new world order" abroad look like more of the same old disorder at home? Color it Yellow. Metastasized neglect, and bankrupt violence.

We keep hearing how we are using American power to enforce the resolutions of the United Nations. Strange . . . haven't seen a blue U.N. flag anywhere.

One of the great World War I poets, Wilfred Owen, who died in the trenches of *that* senseless conflict, looked forward from the battlefields to *The Next War* . . .

. . . when each proud fighter brags He wars on Death
—for lives; not men—for flags."

That is the war we need to fight. Let's color *it* . . . red, white and blue.

Graham Hutchins, Pullman, WA 99163

The Palouse Papers

Machu Picchu

They hid this city
On the tops of the mountains;
Above the gaze of those
Whose greed for gold
Kept their mean and covetous eyes
From lifting their look either to the hills
　　or to God.

And now these ruins,
Emerging from the mists,
Or radiant in the golden sunlight;
Bear witness to no conquistador

116

But time, and this remains a city rare
That never saw the sword
      disturb its peace.

Even to this day those who come upon this place,
And through the lonely gate astride the narrow road;
Are subdued by silence,
Ravished by beauty, and taken captive
To the magnificent crags that
Surround this citadel
      of splendor.

What a wonder to have seen it as it was . . .
When . . . fragrant with flowers,
Her streets filled with running laughter,
The happy souls who lived within these walls
Went forth to till the terraced cliffs,
And reap the harvest of
      their holy grain;

Or bathed in sunburst
And the waterfall,
Witnessed the dancing light,
And sensed the summons of the shadows,
To offer solemn sacrifice
In convocations of the
      invincible Sun.

—from A Word in Season, 1991.

The Paradox of Power

A recent political cartoon shows a huge rhinoceros eyeing an insect. The rhino's horn is painted with stars and stripes, and the insect has a stinger poised to strike the giant beast with deadly venom. The wary rhino could stamp out the insect with its giant hoof in a second. The insect could quickly kill the great beast with deadly poison. A strange power struggle indeed! What does it mean? You guessed it . . . this was the recent face off with Iraq brilliantly interpreted by the cartoonist. These two nations and their leaders all seem to have great strength coupled with incredible weakness. The world is mystified, and asks a lot of questions. Why are the weak so strong? Why are the strong so weak?

We live in a world that worships power. Conversely, we deplore weakness. Signs of weakness in ourselves frighten us, in others anger us, in our nation or world make us insecure, in the human condition itself, perplex us and rob us of hope. We feel powerless in the face of personal, historical or cosmic forces that seem to direct our destiny without our consent.

To compound the problem our reaction to weakness in ourselves or others in our world is often just another demonstration of weakness. Some years ago when struggling with what I perceived to be my own personal inadequacy, a phrase from T. S. Eliot, describing his own vocational and spiritual struggles, practically jumped off the page into my consciousness. The great poet observed that it is:

". . . weakness to be wroth with weakness."

So, our angry reaction to weakness is all too often itself an expression of weakness. We get mad at those who are angry, or at ourselves for lashing out at them! We even worry about those who worry!

The whole world in its struggle and powerlessness cries out for justice, for security, for a better life, for some shred of hope . . . for God. It is basically a longing for wholeness, for strength, for life, for salvation. How can we "win strength out of weakness?" Where can we find God? Is there not some Almighty power that can answer our need, strengthen our feeble hands, confirm our will to righteousness, enable us to live victoriously in a world of so much defeat?

The Christian faith seems to offer no answer here! Our quest for the Almighty leads us to a helpless baby born in a barn. Our longing for goodness and life takes us straight to a cross where the most stunning life ever lived comes to a bloody and scandalous end in a brutal execution. *This?*—is *God?* Ridiculous! How can a child in a manger, a man on a cross, scattered and frightened disciples, answer my need and yours, and the groaning of a world that is discovering the impotence of its power? This faith, far from meeting our need, is itself at its core, "sown in weakness and in dishonor."

But wait, that is but part of the story. Things are not always what they seem! The Cross of Christ exposes the inadequacy of our power but also the power that is made perfect in our weakness. Paul calls it the "foolishness of God which is wiser than men and the weakness of God which is stronger than men."

Since the event of Jesus Christ what the world calls power is seen to be impotence and what the world calls weakness is the occasion for the unveiling of God's power. Invincible love will rule in the end, not coercive might. We are called and enabled to replace our love of power with the power of love!

Let us therefore, when we are tempted to fear or insecurity in the face of weakness; or anger, hostility, or immaturity in ourselves or others; be open to God's strength enabling us to love instead of hate, to forgive instead of resent, to hope instead of despair, to help instead of hurt.

Is not this what our Lenten journey is all about? God's love that was born a helpless baby is destined for a cross? But that cross calls us to gracious forgiveness! And then Easter empowers us to share an incredible joy! When we can see the cross at the cradle and the new birth at the empty tomb, we will win love out of defeat and come to know that "what is sown in weakness will be raised in power," and "what is sown in dishonor will be raised in glory."

We have known a lot of sorrow and anguish in our church and community lately and need some comfort and strength. As we walk with Christ to his cross this Lenten season, may we discover afresh how God can help us win strength out of weakness and joy out of pain. And then . . . we can all sing . . . "let the weak say, 'I am strong,' . . . let the poor say, 'I am rich' . . . because of what the Lord has done for us! Give

Thanks" . . . and echo the Apostle Paul . . . "Thanks be to God . . . who *gives* us the victory through our Lord Jesus Christ!"
Your Pastor, Graham Hutchins

—from *The Messenger*, Simpson United Methodist Church, Pullman, Washington, Lent 1991.

Port Angeles Papers

Nuclear Option?

The use of the term "nuclear option" by the various political establishments in our nation's capital to describe a game of parliamentary one-up-man-ship I find to be highly offensive. Parties on all sides of this political maneuver seem to reveal a profound disconnect between the meanings of terms and their usage.

"Nuclear option" is another instance of Orwellian "newspeak" that euphemistically hides the grim reality of the horrors it really describes. Like "collateral damage" there are a multitude of corpses behind it. We may have forgotten, but the rest of the world remembers, that America is the only nation in history to use nuclear weapons to destroy vast cities of mostly innocent people. We used our newly developed "nuclear" option on Hiroshima and Nagasaki. The results were not parliamentary procedure but a holocaust. And now, as we seek to limit the spread and use of nuclear weapons by others, we are engaged in adding to our nuclear arsenal with tactical "bunker busting" bombs. This is a grim game. The world is watching, and sees us not as the missionaries of democracy but rather as an imperial threat to world peace that trivializes both language and reality.

Glimpses of Village Life . . . in the Heart of the Vast City of Jakarta

We often like to eat a meal on the balcony of the eighth floor of our apartment building in Jakarta. We enjoy this view to the south, looking toward the mountains near Bogor. But what really fascinates us is the life below us in the local *kampong* or urban village, the kind of place where so many of the people in this vast city live. In fact, surrounding the many incredible skyscraper hotels, apartments, government buildings and office towers, as well as its more upscale residential districts, Jakarta is like a great conglomerate of *kampungs*; that together make up this city of probably about 15 to 18 million people. We see a lot of things happening in the *kampong* that we overlook from our balcony. We don't like to feel like some sort of voyeurs spying on people, but we can't help but have a marvelous overview of urban village life that would hardly be possible in any other way.

Right below us, just past the parking lot of this apartment complex, and over a wall and some trees, is a small river, and along its banks and beyond are many homes and other buildings that throb with life, day and night. In the morning we hear the crowing of roosters, and at night during the Moslem festivals the sometimes incessant explosion of firecrackers. [And speaking of roosters, there are some at the gate of our apartment complex. Often when our driver stops to pick up or drop off the entry card, a rooster crosses the street right in front of us, almost as if trained by the guards to keep an eye on the proceedings!]

Directly across from us is a school, in the yard of which children are happily playing between their classes, or having a sort of assembly from time to time. They too, arrive early in the morning, and their cheerful voices are a delight to hear at any hour.

Around us in the heart of this densely populated area are at least a half dozen mosques, from which the Call to Prayer comes five times a day from loudspeakers on their minarets to summon the faithful Moslem population to this holy obligation to Allah. This begins every morning at 4:45 so that no one fails to hear it. And not only is the Call to Prayer heard, but the service itself, with its often haunting chant and sometimes wailing, sometimes soothing, sometimes vigorous rhythms that can in no way be confused with Western music or worship.

The river winds through this community with its paradoxical threat and promise to the lives of those who dwell along its banks. We see people casting nets either to catch fish, or the debris that floats down it that can be recycled into something useful for their families. Children swim in it, and enjoy playing along its banks. The houses are close to the water's edge and often share a common wall with each other. Some are nicer homes, others small and even others have a sort of ramshackle appearance. A few of these even have outhouses built out over the water's edge, with fabric wrapped around it for some semblance of privacy, and perhaps a roof. From our vantage point on the eighth floor we are all too privy to the bathroom habits of some of our neighbors. It is truly a different world.

We have seen the river flood from time to time and once quite heavily, so that even the school was inundated and had to close for three or four days to be cleaned and dried out. Many of the homes along the river bank suffer flooding at these times, but we observe the people cleaning up their yards and sweeping out their houses as if this was just a part of their daily lives that they hardly question.

During the heavier flood we witnessed quite a sense of community below as the people sought to deal with the problems it presented. We saw a woman riding a bicycle that was up to its hubs in water and stopping by to chat with her neighbors. There was much laughter and conversation. At a home nearby, the man of that house was busy caring for his monkeys that had taken refuge on the roof of their cage, while the young mother sitting on the porch suddenly opened her dress to give access to her breast so her young child could climb up on her lap to be fed. An older woman in the background was busy sweeping water out the door of the house. Other children were playing and watching their dad tend to the needs of the monkeys. Meanwhile, nearby, another man is waist deep in the water seeking to catch in a net the various things that are floating by carried on the abundant waters of the flood. He stops to sort his catch, picking out what might be useful, and then returns the rest to the flotsam on the river. At another house, a few doors away from the river, we saw a small boy dive into his front yard as if it had at last become his swimming pool! He seemed as happy as we who swim only a hundred yards away in a magnificent pool we share with residents of the apartment and those marvelous caring frogs we have written about before. A few blocks away in the background is an open space where garbage is dumped, and people scavenge useful items, and then it is burned from time to time, adding its smoke to the often polluted air of this city.

On the other side of our apartment complex is a nice neighborhood, with some lovely homes and streets, beautiful walls and gardens, and nearby a driving range for golfers. To reach our apartments is a narrow street, *Warung Jati Barat* . . . or "Teak Shop West" . . . that is lined with small shops and homes and a magnificent white mosque. Here we see village life every day as we travel to and fro . . . and sometimes we stroll down it and greet the friendly people who live and work there. Here are boys playing ball, food cart vendors plying their wares, people visiting, others going to and from the Mosque, or the bus, or their work. We buy vegetables and fruit from a woman's stand in front of her home. She goes to the market downtown each day very early, perhaps 4 or 5 A.M., and purchases the fresh produce, fish, and chickens she hopes to sell to the neighbors. The other day we were invited into a shop of a man who builds model ships with a crew of young men working at a big table in the sweltering heat. During the week he works for Mobil Oil . . . and his English is quite good. He sends many of these model ships [often oil tankers] to Mobil Oil in New York where they are given to corporate customers.

One day, not too long ago, we needed to get some pictures of various things to send via e-mail to granddaughter Stephanie in the States for a school report. We walked out the little street to the main thoroughfare and took some pictures of buses, families on motorcycles [sometimes four or five on a single cycle], vendor's carts, and the rush of traffic. Suddenly across the highway we saw a man walking in the hot afternoon sun and carrying great bundles on a long bamboo pole over his shoulder extending out for about four feet in front and back of him. Then we noticed that he was not only barefoot, but stark naked! We took his photo and were amazed, when it was developed, that it was taken when he was walking in front of a giant sign for AC . . . Air Conditioning! A few yards further, he stopped under a tree and pulled out a sarong from one of his bags and put it on.

We recently witnessed the Moslem Feast of Sacrifice . . . or *Idyl*

Adha. This in commemoration of Abraham's ancient sacrifice of the ram on Mt. Moriah. [The Quran states that it was Ishmael not Isaac who was spared by the offering of the ram.] Suddenly, for days ahead, this vast urban sprawl of Jakarta was full of goats, oxen and some sheep, which were placed in vacant lots or in parks and fed by men hauling carts of fodder, cut from trees and bushes in yards and cemeteries. Down our little street was a vacant lot, with these animals in it, including a huge horned ox, and kids crowding around to pet, feed and admire them. They were then suddenly all gone in one day, sold to families for their offering on the Day of Sacrifice, slaughtered for the Feast, and the meat then given to the poor. That night the empty lot to the south of us where the garbage is burned was a whole city block of fire, and we surmised that it was a vast incinerator for the remains of the slaughtered animals that could not be used.

A while back, during the month long observance of *Ramadan* . . . where Muslims fast all day from sunup to sundown . . . without even a drink of water in this hot climate . . . we discovered that they make up for it by feasting much of the night. The neighborhood mosques were lively with services broadcast from their loudspeakers, and all around us throughout the entire night was the explosion of countless firecrackers. With the dawn came silence, except for the daily calls to prayer, and the fast resumed. It makes our Christian observance of *Lent* look rather tame indeed.

And so life goes on . . . here in this vast city of villages. We will share later some of the other dimensions of life in this city, including the life of our church, that seeks to make its witness in this multi-dimensional society that is Indonesia.

Jakarta, Indonesia, Lent 2000.

Some Things Are Not Themselves Alone

Some things are not themselves alone,
But signal something greater still,
A flower that grows, the bush that burns,
A tree upon a lonely hill.

124

There is an ocean in your tears,
Delight itself rides on your smile,
A world within your touch resides,
Bright glory in your eyes beguile.

These things are but themselves and more,
Some samples of the things that are,
But you are more than touch or smile,
And closer than things near or far.

How to find the way or words
To render what I want to say?
Things do not speak, or seem to know,
What they themselves convey.

Something in the scheme of things,
Implies a greater whole than they,
Something in the things themselves,
Speaks the words they cannot say.

One day alone can well negate
The reign of universal night,
One smile this date can dissipate
A cloud of overwhelming fright.

A tear might melt a heart of stone,
'Til stones cry out and hearts are won,
The glory in your eyes reveal,
A greater light than can the sun.

These words are but themselves,
And yet, convey another Word to you,
The word of welcome and of Love
That words could never tell, but do.

—from A Word in Season.

The Timid Mr. Bush

We tend to think that our president is bold and brash, and cares less what the world thinks of him. He wants pre-emptive strikes against evil as he perceives it, and believes he knows it when he sees it. He demands that others join him in this crusade, and asserts that "those who are not with us are against us." He is not un-assertive.

But maybe we should look at it again. He is really much too timid. He takes the easy way to resolve conflict instead of the hard way, and commits the age-old mistake of confusing victory with peace. He threatens force and seems eager to use it. A real man seeks to establish community—not to engage in violence, but to stop it.

Leaders don't order, they "lead." Bullies bluster and are really cowards at heart.

If you have a lot of weight to throw around you need to be gentle. If you really carry a big stick, you have all the more obligation to speak very softly. If you are truly "in charge" you might try consensus building without being pressured into it by an anxious world. Real men not only eat quiche, but dare to make peace.

Fear is not the same as respect. Our president and his policies generate more fear than respect in the world. Indeed, most of the world thinks we are the ones who need a regime change, not just Iraq.

If God has blessed America, it is to make us a blessing, not a curse to the world. "Blessed are the peacemakers" was not a description of the timid. And in this kind of world it looks to be the only realism.

May God help us.

The Water Journey

The road wound over the back of the island and down into a small valley toward the sea. We stopped by the ruins of an old church that lay behind a gate and near a "burn," or stream. Under the watchful eye of some Highland cattle on the opposite bank we entered the door of the roofless little church that stood so alone in this quiet valley at the foot of the mountain. It was obvious that the church had been there a very long time and it seemed that in the evening light we could almost listen to the silent choir of the stones that sang of the past . . . of beginnings remote . . . of the morning of this world by this radiant northern sea.

In the middle of these ruins was a stone baptismal font, an eloquent witness to a New World yet to be—to the meeting place of this ancient world and the world to come—to life and death and washing and renewal. We were aware that we shared some understanding of the "how" and the "why" of these ancient acts and we wondered about who was baptized there, and when. The old stone font was now probably only filled when it rained on this roofless church, and the only "baptisms" were of the birds that could dip into its waters. It was a fitting symbol both of the past and the future, of a dead world and a new life. A symbol that seemed almost as ancient as the stone of which it was made, and as new as the life that it promised.

We took some photographs there of our hosts and listened as they told of how this church had been built here centuries ago in honor of the landing of St. Columba down on the beach where this stream merged with the sea. He had sailed from Ireland with his followers in their little boats and had landed here with an eye to settling and building and starting the work of bringing a New World of faith to an ancient and pagan people. He then climbed the nearby mountain and found he could still see the Irish coast from its summit. Having taken a vow never to return to Ireland, and thinking as well that this backward look would make his disciples homesick, he decided to push on out of sight of that old world from which they had so recently come. So he gathered up his little band of companions and sailed on over the horizon to Iona.

As our friends finished this story and we were returning to their car, we suddenly noticed in the evening sky, shining in the sun, so high it was beyond hearing, with a long vapor trail streaming behind it, a jetliner winging its way eastward from another "new world" to an old. It was an astonishing contrast: the old stone church, the silent cattle, the whisper of the wind and the past; and high above us in the golden sky . . . in the long northern twilight . . . this shining emissary from a new world that Columba could never have imagined, crossing an entire ocean in less time than it took his little boats to cross the strait from Ireland.

It was a moment fit only for silence . . . and wonder. We too were from that new world across the sunlit northern sea. We had come here from out of those western skies to see these friends in this "old world" of ancient stones and voyages, tales of adventure, and a common faith. And it was this, the common faith that had brought us together. Without it we would never have met to share a ministry, nor embarked on such journeys as we did, and discovered together in the luminous evening of this day how so many stories and worlds, memories and dreams, arrivals and departures, converged upon this place. And yet, in all its variety, it is, in a sense, one story. A story of water, and faith, and our common journey. The old font, the stream, the sunlit sea, the river of time and of meaning, the meetings and partings and visions and dreams, seemed to flow into and out of each other like a meandering stream that is nonetheless a river of no return. The faith that brought Columba to this place had brought us together. Because of our common baptism, understanding, purpose and communion, we had become friends and companions who shared the great story of where we had come from, and where we were going—of old worlds and new, and journeys and crossings, and the call of the sea.

The Sea is in us. We were born in water. We came out of the Flood; we escaped through the Sea. We came over the River. We were washed in the Fountain. We escape death by drowning. We drink living water, fresh from the Tomb.

The Journey is in us, too. And we are on a Journey. We came over the horizon of chaos on an ark of grace. We came through the wilderness, and went on to the conquest. We built and expanded, failed and heard warnings, fell in our pride and ended in ruins. We went into Exile, and wept and remembered. We recovered our faith and returned with rejoicing. Our call is to follow. We are commissioned to go. To go into all the world. To go toward a *New World*. Out of the Flood, and through the deep waters, over the River, the desert, the seas, into the darkness, the dawning, the daylight, singing and shouting, kicking and screaming, laughing and crying, loving and dying, dreaming, and daring, doing and failing, arriving . . . departing. We are on the Journey . . . in little boats, with tired feet, soaring over oceans, climbing the hills. On to the horizons, into the sunset, on to the City beyond the great Sea . . .

And so it was, on a luminous evening, these worlds converged at an old stone font, in a roofless church, by a little stream and some watching cattle, on an island in the Hebrides, where the landing place of an ancient saint is daily crossed by a jetliner's flight.

Back here, a year later, by this great Western sea even vaster than the Atlantic, in this "new world" where I live, I heard that my friend in that "old world" had crossed over the Sea. He has gone on ahead to the world that is new. Not here, where I live, but to that City *beyond* the Sea.

Our memories are rich of times we shared together—of our common dreams, and work, and many good conversations . . . and of a last luminous evening with a good and faithful friend. We are glad we have a photograph of that time when he stood with his wife in the roofless old church with their hands resting on that ancient stone font—where the world is concluded—and the Journey begins.

—after hearing of the death of the Rev. Willie Dundas, Ferndale, Washington, 1979.

On Thankfulness

One of the great historic confessions of the Christian church is the *Heidelberg Catechism* written in the sixteenth Century. It has three main sections that reflect the understanding in the church at that time of the state of the world and the response of faith within it. The three sections are: I, Of Man's Misery. II, Of Man's Redemption and III, Of Thankfulness

I. Of Man's Misery: Sound like our world? To read the newspapers or watch the evening news is to be aware of the misery and bondage that still keep the world in the iron grip of evil. It is a world of fear, hostility,

129

war, and crime and violence. Even many of the ways in which we seek to stop or prevent evil seem to bring on more evil. We call terrorists "Freedom Fighters"—or vice versa. We call aggressive behavior "national security" or "defense." We call the exploitation of our natural resources "free enterprise" and then call weapons of death "resources." On Man's Misery indeed!

Happily, there are other realities in the world that confront us. Such as the good news about God in the gospel witness of Christ.

II. Of Man's Redemption: . . . the great confession of faith calls it. Thus the writers of that statement of faith confronted both the tragic human predicament of our need and the incredible divine resource of God's grace. The one responded to by the other was not an extension of either pessimism about the human situation or a naive optimism about God. But rather a response that saw how God's gift transformed the human dilemma and issued in a life of gratitude. The hallmark of the Christian life is gratitude. The misery of man, and the redemption God provides result in a people whose lifestyle is one of gratitude. This is astonishing! And very relevant today. Thoreau once noted that most people live lives of what he called "quiet desperation." This is true today too, is it not? Except for many, the desperation is hardly quiet. An age of assassins and terrorists is desperate but not too quiet about it.

III. Of Thankfulness: Maybe we need to count our blessings again. We might find good reason to live a life of quiet thankfulness. As we celebrate again that great American holiday called Thanksgiving, perhaps we should reflect a bit, and discover what people of faith did in the sixteenth Century and conclude that in spite of all the human misery we can take note of each day, that the final assessment of it all should nonetheless be "On Thankfulness."

—Thought for the Day #2, November 21, 1987, *The Pullman Herald*
Graham Hutchins, Pastor, Simpson United Methodist Church.

The Palouse—Summer's End

By day and night
The great machines of harvest,
Fulfilling their annual purpose,
Lay their corduroy patterns on the land.
The silent fields are stubble now,
Beneath the scudding clouds.
The golden wheatscape—and the summer heat—
The giant combines wrenching pasta from the hills—
Will now give way to the
Crisp autumn and its tasks,
Days of plowing and planting,
Storing and selling,
And all the preparations for another crop.
The proud elevators groan with grain
That waits to ride the tides
Of market to the world,
As this lonely land will once again
Feed multitudes under other skies than these.

The students come from far and near—
The future?—a distant purpose in their eyes—
Or merely a wishing for the weekend and its fun.
Their families somehow start to seem
The stuff of memories,
And home perhaps a place to call for funds.
But for now, it's
Football and frenzy,
Pledging and playing,
Research, writing, the seminar,
Libraries and labs,
Study or sleeping,
Now, and then, or later—

New friends, old problems,
New problems, old friends—
The hunt for housing, or parking,
Parties and pizza—
And traffic jams in a vast land,
With not a freeway in sight.

We, who would share these days with them,
Should dream and plan and pray,
And greet the stranger, student, friend,
With warmth and welcome,
As we prepare for other kinds of harvest.
So let us work, and wait, and harbor hope,
And do the deeds of careful nurture
Leading toward the ripening promise
Of the future and its golden grain.

—from A Word in Season.

The Palouse Papers

On Tedium . . . and the *Te Deum*

The traffic starts to snarl again in its usual twice-daily gridlock on the Palouse. The streets are filling up with students. Travelers appear with foreign landscapes in their eyes and memories. The harvest is about finished. There is a touch of coolness in the evening. Rooms are being rented. U-Hauls appear on the scene. New faces ask directions. We rush about trying to get in a few more summer activities before the busy round of autumn . . . [what was that word? . . . "autumn?" . . . that's right! Fall! Here it comes!] The groans you hear may be your own! "But where did summer go?" we say. And yet, we say it with ambivalence. We see the frenzy coming and are filled with both dread and excitement.

With nostalgia for the fleeting days of summer and in anticipation of what the coming months might bring. How *should* we look at it? With dread? Or excitement? With anticipation or despair? As an impending tedium? . . . Or, in perhaps some other way?

One of the great ancient canticles or songs of the Church has a title that sounds like "tedium" . . . but it really means the opposite. It's called the *Te Deum laudamus*, which is a gracious Latin phrase that means . . . *We praise thee, Oh God!* . . . To praise God is not *tedium* . . . but *Te Deum* . . . In spite of how you felt when your parents made you sit through church as a child! Sometimes, what looks like "tedium" hides within it the rich possibilities of *Te Deum*! Like our work. Or our busy schedules. Or our daily round of household duties. Or our social obligations in the community. Or our spiritual need to nurture one another in the faith.

We built a nation where we all affirm and want to claim the "inalienable right" to the "pursuit of happiness." Too many have discovered only the tedious loneliness of their desperate lives. Do we need to rediscover the *Te Deum* of life? The extraordinary opportunity that lurks in the routine features of our days? The high privilege that is ours in having work to do and energy to do it? Of having others to share our tasks and burdens and joys? Do you really want summer to go on forever? Right now the coming frenzy may look like tedium. Let's make it sound and seem and be the occasion of *Te Deum* . . . a reason for praise to God for the great opportunities of work and service and fellowship that are granted us in this place and time.

As our year of activities begins here in this congregation of God's people called to serve in the name of Christ in this busy university town . . . let's be glad we can be a *Te Deum* people! Who even get to welcome a new hymnal, and a new organist/choir director to enable us to sing the praise of God together in a "new song" that the world may see and hear and sing as well.

Here it comes! The *Te Deum* . . . ! "*We praise thee, Oh God, we acknowledge thee to be the Lord . . .*"

Sing it!

Your pastor . . . "Hutch"

—from *The Messenger*, Simpson United Methodist Church, Pullman, Washington, 8/90.

An Amazing Spectacle of the Birth of Democracy in a Muslim Land

Greetings from Indonesia!—October 1999

We have just witnessed a very historic set of events here in Jakarta! An amazing spectacle of a nation emerging at last from dictatorship and corruption into a democratic process of governance that most of us in the Western world take all too much for granted.

The MPR, or Peoples Legislative Assembly for Indonesia, meeting in special assembly as the Peoples Consultative Assembly even had to write the procedural rules under their decades old Constitution to facilitate the *election* of their first president on Wednesday and vice president today. These were the first leaders of the nation who did not assume power by coup or default or abuse of power.

It has been amazing to watch! All of this has culminated in the last three days! To watch the faces of the legislators on TV you can tell they are for the first time enjoying the exercise of freedom to vote their conscience apart from party coercion or bribery or whatever. Generals step down, winners are magnanimous, losers are graciously accepting defeat. There was some disruption last night after Megawati Sukarnoputri, the daughter of the founder of the nation five decades ago lost the presidency in the vote in the Assembly even though she is clearly the peoples candidate and won the popular vote by a plurality in the general election in June by thirty-three percent. The winner was a Muslim cleric . . . a highly respected nearly blind old man of fifty-nine [!] who is the leader of the largest Muslim organization in the world, but who idolizes Mahatma Gandhi and really upset a lot of people awhile back by saying Indonesia should recognize Israel because after all they mostly believe in God whereas the country has recognized a number of states that are officially atheist! He says it jokingly and graciously and like a certain politician brother-in-law of mine tells them all to go to hell and enjoy the trip!

It is astonishing! Former-president Habibie went on for over three hours the other night before the Parliament trying to justify his brief administration since the fall of Soeharto, and the Parliament rejected it. [Many of them were falling asleep . . . as I did after 11:30 P.M. and some interrupted him [unheard of impunity in the past . . . you'd have been taken out and shot . . . or just "disappeared."] Anyway, the new president, "Gus Dur," [his nickname . . . means Elder Brother] [Dory informs me now that his real name is Adurrahman Wahid] . . . (no wonder he has a nickname!) won and didn't even run for the office! . . . and then reached out to his friend Megawati who he defeated and thanked her for her amazing contribution to their joint victory for democracy in this country. Today, she was elected vice president and in another half-hour will be sworn in, as he was last night! [None of this waiting three months for Inauguration Day sort of jazz!]

The MPR/PCC also passed on the night before the election recognition of the right of East Timor to govern itself according to the election held there in May under UN auspices and that has had such disastrous consequences by the militia and insubordinate factions of the Indonesian Army. People didn't even dare talk politics here only two years ago. And now they are probably going to celebrate the fact that this fourth largest country in the world has at long last joined the ranks of democratic nations. They will probably prove once again Churchill's dictum that "democracy is the worst form of government in the world . . . except for all those other systems." Dory and I have watched all this in amazement. From the students in the streets to the legislators in the Assembly to talking with people [such as our delightful and devout Muslim driver] and listening to the BBC and the CNBC [out of Hong Kong and Singapore] and even the local stations in Bahasa [language] Indonesia who have been airing the whole thing. The vote was tallied in front of everyone with IIII\\ on a big board. A cliffhanger to watch! Today there weren't even any traffic problems in this city . . . of millions of cars and even more people . . . the whole nation was glued to their television sets!

And so it goes . . . we will now have tea and speak of absurdities and then go watch the inauguration of Mrs. Megawati as vice president of Indonesia!

PS: Dory just read to me from the newspaper . . . *The New York Herald Tribune International Edition for Asia* . . . that a common joke in Indonesia is that there are three things you can never be certain about: Life—Death—and "Gus Dur"!

135

A cartoon in another English language paper here . . . the *Observer* . . . has Habibie . . . Megawati, and "Gus Dur" as hear no evil, see no evil and speak no evil. Habibie was deaf to a lot of stuff . . . Dur can't see . . . and Megawati never seems to speak!

PPS: . . . Later: Just watched Megawati's inauguration and heard her inaugural address. Incredible! She was almost electrifying. Often accused of not saying anything she spoke like she does it all the time! Powerful speaker. Lifted up all the themes of the nation and called on everyone to pitch in and help make it happen. Reminds me of Lincoln's great line . . . "that this nation might have a new birth of freedom." Her father, the nation's founder Sukarno, was deposed by Soeharto in a coup in the '70s . . . putting her into limbo! She only has a high school education . . . yet grew up in the Presidential Palace here in Jakarta . . . Got her party wrecked a few years ago. Then started a new one and pulled it off. She even thanked the students in the streets for their role and told them now to go back to work and study . . . "Your Mother," she said, "is standing before you!" Amien Raiz . . . the Speaker of the Assembly, then closed the session and also thanked the demonstrating students . . . [He organized them a couple of years ago to overthrow Soeharto! He has a PhD in political science from the University of Chicago.] This is an incredible week here in Jakarta!

. . . As you can see . . . politics around here is hardly boring!

—Graham & Dory Hutchins

P.S. . . . Herewith a poetic reflection on all this:

Jakarta, October 1999

Seeing
They were in need of vision
They elected a blind man
To lead them into a brighter future;
And a silent queen mother,
Whose daddy founded the nation,

To nurture their people
Into the dignity
Of freedom.
Sensing,
Against all odds,
That he would get the job anyway,
He didn't even run for the office.
Knowing she had the people with her,
She kept her peace.
And now this odd couple
Plan to conquer the greed
That brought their nation down,
So hurting the people;
While the world watches
Wondering,
If this is truly
A matahari terbit*
For this land.

*Here in Indonesia they call the sun "the eye . . . *Mata* . . . of the day" . . . *Hari* . . .
  Matahari Terbit = sunrise.

O Christ, Who Wept Beside the Tomb of Lazarus

Tune: Vicar 11 10. 11 10. #178 UM Hymnal

1. O Christ, who wept beside the tomb of Lazarus,
   In sorrow, anger, and in holy love,
   Help us to see your glory in our anguish,
   Now speak your word of life to all that grieve.

2. O Lord, with thanks, you lifted eyes to heaven,
   To One who works the will of Love in you,
To do the deed that showed to us your glory,
   And brought from death the one you held so dear.

3. O God of help, who in your Son has promised
   Eternal life to all who will believe,
Show us in Christ, your will at last accomplished,
   That death might die, and all the world might live.

4. Raise us again to life once more, like Lazarus,
   Cry out your word so able to remove
The grip of death and all the fear that binds us,
   Make us today a sign of your great love.

5. Summon from sleep all we that lie in darkness,
   In unbelief, like death, that holds us fast.
Free us to hear your voice and sing your praises,
   Lift us afresh to life that's new at last.

—*Hymns for All Seasons and Other Hymns.* Note: Lazarus, in Hebrew, means,
One whom God helps . . .

The Port Angeles Papers

Honoring a Heritage—Desecration or Dedication?

Letter to the Editor
The Peninsula Daily News
12-17-04
Honoring the Heritage
The graving yard project in Port Angeles harbor has inadvertently

uncovered the graves of Klallam ancestors, and the ancient village of Tse-whit-zen.

The tragic impasse in this situation cries out for reconciliation of all parties involved, living and dead, past, present and future and the communities that reside in this beautiful place together.

Can we not honor our past without burying our future? To avoid the desecration of the graves of ancestors, can we not rededicate them to sustaining the prosperity of their descendents?

The world exhibits many civilizations built one upon another in which the past is revered and the future achieved side by side.

Could the Elwha people honor their ancestors by rededicating the place where they rest to a Tse-whit-zen Graving Dock built on the graves of an ancient people that participate with their descendents and neighbors in constructing a strong, sustainable future of prosperity and community?

The structure itself might have a great stone of commemoration, dedicating the place to proudly building bridges to the future on the remains and memories of the past.

Nearby there could be a stunning visitors center displaying the rediscovered cultural heritage of the Klallam tribe—"The Strong People"—in all its ancient richness, with some replicated Tse-whit-zen dwellings giving a sense of the village life of those who came before.

Graham Hutchins
Port Angeles

—Note: *The Graving Yard Project* undertaken by the Washington State Department of Transportation in the harbor of Port Angeles was to build the pontoon structures for the refurbishing of the Hood Canal Bridge, a major highway facility connecting the Olympic Peninsula with the Puget Sound Basin. The excavation for the construction site uncovered a major archeological heritage and many remains of ancestors of the Elwha tribe of the Klallam People dating back some 2,700 years. This led to the halting and cancellation of the project as cited above.

The Church Stands in the Heart of the City, Part 1

The Church stands in the heart of the city. Or should we say in one of the city's hearts. For this is a city of cities . . . a vast conglomerate of humanity that is really at least five cities in one, each with its own government and centers and life.

The church we speak of has been there for years, and was once surrounded by green fields we are told. Now it is threatened by a shopping mall that generates incredible traffic beside it day and night, engulfing it in exhaust fumes, car calls and an expanding consumer frenzy. Towering over the churchyard the mall's ten-story additions now under construction wrap around the church property like a great monster jaw threatening to swallow it whole in one giant gulp. The land the church stands on is itself coveted by the developers of the mall but its property and location were designated the church's right of possession by the first president and founder of the Republic . . . though rumor has it that the documents to that effect have mysteriously disappeared recently from the bank vault.

The Church has an impressive history, program, and presence in the heart of this city. It boasts a membership of several thousand, an on site clinic for its members and the unfortunate, a social witness of justice and compassion in a society that needs both in large amounts, a thriving church school and youth program, a staff of dozens, from clergy to officers of administration and secretaries, to security guards and custodians, and a session of elders that devote a great deal of time to the ongoing mission and program of the congregation. It not only serves the population of its own people, but sponsors on site three congregations of foreign groups who reside in this capital city but gather in this place to worship in their own languages: Korean, German and English.

We have been involved in one of these congregations that attracts expatriate English-speaking people from all over the world including those of Indonesia itself who have lived abroad or are married to those who have come here to live and work.

We share in the amazing setting, situation and challenge the larger indigenous church, the Ephatha congregation of the Church of West Java faces. Our future too, is threatened; not just by the mall, but by the culture, by the transience of the expatriate community, and by the tendency to despair, facing the problems of being the church in such a place. And yet, our congregation is full of gifted and committed people that love their church and its mission and want to see it recover from its decline during the national "crisis" of a couple of years ago, which saw many foreigners leave due to the political instability that brought with it economic uncertainty.

The English-speaking congregation now has an office in the former residence of the previous Pastor, and has hired a full-time secretary who speaks both English and Indonesian and is able to be a central focus of communication and coordination for the activities of the fellowship. There is new life and activity and a growing sense of community among the people that is a joy to behold. New programs were started and events held, like during Holy Week, that have been well received and awakened the people to new possibilities for their life together.

This has led us to have a variety of experiences in both the church and the city that have been rich, disturbing, challenging, hopeful, and full of mystery and wonder as we sought to be the church in this dynamic and amazing city of incredible contrast, energy, diversity and problems. Here are some more vignettes of our life here that might help you understand what our situation has been.

The aunt of the bride-to-be came to us requesting a wedding for her niece in the near future. The fiancée was from Wales and currently working in Australia on construction sites. He had met this lovely Indonesian woman last year in Bali, and now they were wanting to get married. In order to wed this Indonesian young woman, a Christian, he was required by Indonesian law to be a Christian himself and therefore needed to be baptized. He said he had no religious training whatsoever growing up in Wales.

We met with this couple and arranged for both the baptism and the wedding. Due to the pressure of schedule and accessibility and the need to get it taken care of so they could leave for Wales and find work for the groom, we baptized him on Palm/Passion Sunday as part of an enacted sermon. Two of us read the *Passion According to Mark* and then I preached a brief sermon and called him up to be baptized at its conclusion. I told him that he was sort of like the centurion at the foot of the cross he had just heard about in the *Passion* narrative. This soldier for Rome found himself required to work the dirty duty of executing criminals, and in the course of his having to be there encountered a man on a cross that was strangely different. This soldier, who was neither a Jew nor a disciple, suddenly found himself confessing that this dying Jesus man must truly be a Son of God. His is the true confession at the end of Mark's Gospel where the disciples had betrayed, denied, and deserted Jesus to die alone on the cross. We in the Jakarta Community Church welcomed this young man from Wales into a new humanity, and pointed out to him and all assembled that the hands laid in blessing on his head were the hands of an Australian, an Indonesian, and an American, but even more, they were the hands of those who had discovered for themselves that the man on that cross was indeed, as the Roman soldier had confessed . . . truly the Son of God.

We planned a Service of the Upper Room for Holy Thursday. The Fellowship and Nurture Committee under Dory's direction worked very hard and had a wonderful time preparing the tables for a supper of soup, fruit and bread. Colorful batik runners adorned the tables and there was a bowl to wash each other's hands, and the people engaged in this with joy and a spirit of sharing. I had hoped we might get about thirty people out. We had sixty and they seemed to be quite satisfied not only with the meal but also with the service surrounding it where we sang and shared how the Lord's supper was given to us from a Last Supper Jesus shared with his disciples. This was followed by a glorious Easter celebration with the Altar Table arrayed in gold and white orchids purchased at the early morning flower market nearby on Saturday by Dory and a wonderful Indonesian member of our church . . . Maria Waworuntu, a professor in the university and a radiant lady full of gracious deeds on behalf of the church.

The call came at about 8:45 at night . . . A woman who had been in church that morning told us her mother had just died, and could we come and be with her and a few friends for a while. Fortunately our driver Paul had stayed with us for dinner, and we were able to leave immediately for another part of the city to answer this call for the presence of the church at the time of death. We entered the compound where this woman lived and found her home and were ushered in to meet some neighbors there and then gathered by the body of the dead woman where we sat in silence and prayed together in terms of thanksgiving, commendation and comfort for all concerned.

Those of us gathered by this bed of death were a Serbian Orthodox, a Roman Catholic, a Baptist, two Methodists and a Unitarian. The servants, who are Muslim, waited in the background in silent and reverent respect as this little microcosm of the Church commended an old woman to God and found comfort in the hope that is set before us. Later, as we left, I said to the gracious daughter of the deceased that it might sound strange, but it had been a joy to be there with them that evening.

The La Paz Papers

Some People of La Paz

His name is Carlos . . . He is a fascinating character and friend. He studied law in Bolivia and accounting in America. He is brilliant. He has spent several years as a "volunteer" while trying to help his people, especially those on the *Altiplano*, that vast intermountain plateau between the high ranges of the Andes. Carlos helps them to better their lives in various types of community and economic organizations. He is in conversation with those high up in government and those who live the simple but increasingly complex lives of the peasants in the *campos* of this country.

He refuses to join the political actions of those who confront the government with blockades and protests. He tries to encourage his people to form cooperatives to improve the economic conditions in which they live. For example, he has formed a dairy cooperative on the

Altiplano of hundreds of farmers. To do this he got a grant from the Church of Denmark to raise funds from foundations in America and Europe of some 50 million dollars. The lives and well being of the dairy farmers in the Altiplano have improved immensely. Needless to say, he has not only many friends but enemies on both the left and the right, within the government and among the more radical *campasino* population. He is a charming, fun loving and dynamic guy. He is Catholic but attends our congregation as well as the Roman Church. He rides his bicycle everywhere . . . even out to distant parts of the Altiplano.

Mario is old and suffering from a fall on a construction accident last year. His dark eyes brighten under his shock of black hair, when he learns that the Pastor has come to visit him. He loved to attend church, but is not able to get out much anymore. He sits in his chair in his lovely home in the bright sunshine and gladly joins in conversation with his guests. He comes from Potosí . . . [pronounced *Poe*-toe—see] the highest city in the world, and one of the oldest and richest cities. It is the place where the Spanish discovered silver in what became known as the *Cerro Rico* . . . "the rich hill" and mined enough silver it is said to build a bridge from here to Spain. Others have pointed out that you could also build as long a bridge over the dead bodies of those the Spanish put to work in the mines, including slaves from Africa. Their descendants are the black population of Bolivia, who now live in a couple of towns in the jungle *departments* of the country, having escaped not only the harsh labor in mines, but also the frigid temperatures of the high altitude of Potosí.

At one time Potosí was larger than London. Having grown up in Potosí this fascinating Aymara man went to America and studied to become a mining engineer, and is a graduate of the Colorado School of Mines. He proudly shared stories of his life with me and the parishioner couple who had brought me there to visit with him. His wife, Elsa, who is from Argentina, graciously served us refreshments and they told of their children, one a graduate of the London School of Economics and the other son a graduate of Dartmouth and now in Madrid, Spain, studying medicine. He was so delighted with our visit he seemed to glow with new life and energy, and became more articulate both in Spanish and English as the minutes passed by . . . We finally had to leave and said a prayer and he said good-bye with moist eyes and a marvelous smile.

We need your prayers for a family in our congregation here who are facing an enormous challenge. The husband is a brilliant young attorney, with a lovely American wife. They have three daughters and a son. The girls are often acolytes in our Sunday service, and their mother is on the church board. She is Protestant and he is a Bolivian Catholic. Next Monday, August 6, the national holiday equivalent to our July 4th, he is going to be sworn in as the president of Bolivia, as the current president is dying of cancer and coming home from Walter Reed Hospital in Washington, D.C., to resign because of his health. Jorge Quiroga is facing a huge challenge not only in the country, but also within his own party. As vice president of Bolivia he was part of a coalition government that was tenuous at best, and now as the new president he will face economic crisis, political turmoil, and civil unrest. He is one of the young, dynamic leaders of the country that want to see Bolivia thrive and prosper into a new future . . . but he faces a tremendous task of leadership and struggle to enable his government to succeed.

She is a lovely lady born in Bolivia, but is sort of a world citizen. In fact, she is the Consular Representative in Bolivia for Cyprus, that island nation of fractious Greeks and Turks in the Eastern Mediterranean. She manages and owns a nursing home here in La Paz and another in a city in the north of the country. She cares greatly for her patients and urges her staff to consider their work a ministry to the old and infirm with whom they work and she spends many hours personally seeing to the quality of care and showing love and concern for the individuals dependent on these giving persons for their lives and well being.

He was probably about twelve to fourteen years old and was busy shining shoes in the Plaza Abaroa in the Sopocachi barrio of La Paz. We were walking through the busy plaza and stopped a few moments. Dory realized her shoes needed a shine and we engaged this industrious young lad to do the job. We asked him what he charged to make sure we had enough cash on us to pay him. He answered one *Boliviano* . . . which in $U.S. amounted to a mere fifteen cents. He cheerfully worked on Dory's shoes with great energy and then indicated he would do mine. I agreed, even though they were not in need of a shine just yet. While he worked we indicated in our rough Spanish that he probably was aware that the newly elected President of Peru was once a shoeshine boy like he was today. He was aware of that and seemed to appreciate the comment. We paid him his two Bs for the shines plus whatever few more coins we had at the time, and he thanked us with real warmth and went back to his seat on the park bench where he could watch some other boys playing with a soccer ball. It was a delightful encounter with one of the 800,000 children in this country that have to work for a living. Happily, there is now an agency that is not trying to do away with child labor here [an impossibility in this culture], but are succeeding in regulating it to the point where these kids get help with schooling and health care and opportunity to better their lives in ways their meager incomes would not allow. As for us, we cannot forget this young worker and his smile and eager industry in seeing that our shoes were as bright as his attitude.

On another side of the plaza we were approached by an elderly and nearly blind woman . . . a Chola . . . of many years. Many such women subsist by begging and so we gave her some coins. She persisted in speaking to us, and finally a small boy nearby who was observing the scene tried to help us understand in Spanish that she was trying to tell us something else . . . It turned out she was selling *queso,* a word we then recognized as "cheese." We watched her unwrap the wheels of cheese from the great colorful aguaya on her back and we bought one to take home. We were most impressed and delighted at her persistence and the helpfulness of the boy who even assisted her in making change for us since her old and nearly blind eyes could not quite accomplish the task. She didn't want a handout, but rather longed to participate in the life of the community and to provide for herself.

A Dialogue of Surprise

. . . Or Should We Say . . . A Graceful Conversation Overheard on All Saints Day!

"Something is happening in our congregation! There is a stirring of life that threatens to amaze us! We are planning for a future that we cannot see! We are having visions in the night of programs and ministry that widen our concern and focus our energies. Why there's talk of launching our mission into the future!"

"Not just maintaining our ministry as in the past?"

"We are building the launch pad right here in old Three Forks . . . and modern Pullman . . . right here at Cape Simpson!"

"How did it happen?"

"God knows!"

"Right!"

"Maybe so! It's happening in some strange places . . . like the Finance Committee!"

"But those guys are supposed to be hard-nosed keepers of the status quo . . . a reality check on the sentimental dreamers who are slightly out of touch with the facts of fiscal faithfulness! Not visionaries! Dreamers on the Finance Committee?! You've got to be kidding! Call Nominations! We made a mistake!"

"But Education is in on it too! They are supposed to be running the Sunday School not having grandiose revelations of the Twenty-first Century!"

"What about Nurture? And Worship?"

"They're on board as well and making big plans! So is Outreach! Mission is going to take place!"

"What's the congregation going to do about all this?"

"The excitement is contagious! I think they'll catch it!"

"I bet the Devil won't like it! Amazing!"

"Yeah! Like *Amazing Grace* sort of kicks you into the future! You gotta share the joy!"

"Like all the saints did!"

"What is going on around here?"

"Faith happens!"

"Holy hilarity!"

"So be it!" "Alleluia!"

—All Saints 1990 and counting!

Dear Paper Trails People . . .

Some of you are expecting to hear from us, as we have been in conversation about the possibilities of our going to live in Africa for a year or so. To others this will be "out of nowhere" and [into Africa!] news!

Dory and I flew last weekend to Minneapolis-St. Paul to interview for a position in East Africa with an international congregation similar to the ones we served in Indonesia and Bolivia. It was a great interview and we are delighted to tell you that we have been invited to go to Arusha, Tanzania, sometime within the next month or two to work with the Arusha Community Church, an English-speaking congregation, with expatriates from many other lands including Africans.

We are excited about working with this congregation of missionaries, medical practitioners, educators, UN Personnel, international service organization workers, business people and their families. The people in the church have built a beautiful and functional building and are participating in building a hospital next to the church. They have an active dedicated program to minister to the many needs of the region.

The church council is in the process of helping us secure a visa, which is a somewhat complicated process, since we will be working in the country. They are also finding us appropriate housing and ways of meeting other needs as we all identify them. Arusha is about a mile above sea level, in a temperate climate, where coffee and bananas and other fruits and vegetables are grown. It is also the place from which many safaris go into the Serengeti and climbers come to ascend nearby Mt. Kilimanjaro, the highest mountain in Africa.

We are certainly going to miss our friends and family here and all the good times we have in this beautiful part of the world, but time will go fast and we will return to share with you the excitement of our work and mission in Africa.

There is much to tell about Tanzania, we are learning a great deal by reading but know we will be saturated with new knowledge, once we get there. We would love to share our experiences with friends and family. We will be sending reports about our life and work there, with impressions and stories from time to time. If you would be interested in receiving them, please let us know. We will count on the miracle of email to keep us in touch and would be very happy to hear from any and all of you about life here at home. So *Paper Trails* is about to begin a new venue of musings on the strange wanderings of its author. Maybe I am a "circuit writer" in the "Traveling Ministry" to adapt the use of the Methodist terminology.

Thank you for your patience and attentiveness to this year-and-a-half or more of my memories and reflection in *Paper Trails*. And thank you for your words of appreciation and encouragement. I now have a book of about 120 pages or more . . . if I took the time to look for a publisher! Good thing we are leaving town . . . was just about to run out of material! Guess we'll have to write some more! Meanwhile . . . there's one or two yet to come!

Until later! *Kwa heri* (good-bye in Swahili, the language of Tanzania).

The Port Angeles Papers

The Eternal Tide of Time

Our lives seem to get busier all the time! Even as the calendar year winds down we find more to do to keep us busy! In a very few weeks we must observe Thanksgiving and get our Christmas shopping done. In even less time than that there are papers to be written or read, exams to be given or graded, yards to take care of, meetings to attend, appointments to be kept, deadlines to meet, yesterday's high resolves to complete to-day . . . and on and on it goes.

Did you ever feel like you were running out *of* time? "Time and tide wait for no one" . . . is the time honored conventional wisdom. It is true. Our minutes, hours, days, weeks and years hasten into the waiting future. Or is it the devouring past? Sometimes we wonder if we will ever catch up . . . to say nothing of getting ahead.

Our ancestors fixed their minds on eternity and spent their time preparing to "glorify God and enjoy him forever." For them, eternity was absolute. This life was as the "flower of the field" that fades before the hot wind from the desert. Their days were as grass, but they could celebrate that the word of their God would abide forever.

Our culture makes time absolute. "Time is of the essence," we say, meaning it is of supreme importance. A friend drops by and says "Got time for a cup of coffee?" "Of course not" we say, and sit down to have a cup anyway. We confess that we don't "have" the time, but we "take time" or "make time" for what we really want to do.

We speak of two different kinds of time here. The inexorable march of hours that "wait for no one." And the choice to use the hours in some creative or renewing way. So we are always running out of time, but always taking time to do what really concerns us most. In this tension lies the source of much human creativity that results in the imaginative use of a diminishing resource. "Quality" time is more significant to us than "dead time," the empty time between the creative moments of our lives. Time can be packed with meaning like a sonnet. Or say it all, like the Lord's prayer. Or it can be as dull as bureaucratic prose, and tell as little about the meaning of life as the phone book.

Around Thanksgiving, as the calendar year winds down, much of the Christian church begins anew its liturgical observance of the Christian year. We celebrate in Advent that coming of God into our time to share with us in the limits of our brief lives the beauty and power of the life of God. This is God taking time for us. God, who has all eternity to enjoy, entering into our world that is always running out of time so that our time might be taken up into the significance of God's eternity. In the event of Christ, we discover that God too, knows what it means to "be running out of time" with a mission to accomplish, and a work to be done while it is day, for night comes when no one can work.

Does God in Christ suffer the limits of our *quantity* of time in order to share with us in time the *quality* of God's eternity? An old hymn tells us to "Take time to be holy . . ." Christmas is coming . . . when God "took time" to be worldly, and blessed us with love.

"Time and tide wait for no one." I look out the window of my study toward the Strait and can't tell whether the tide is in or out, but I do know that it will be flooding in again, and "right on time"! The "eternal" sea will see to that. Kind of like our busy days and years isn't it? The tide of time rolls on, when we will have a new flood of days in which to serve and praise the eternal God who has come to us "in the fullness of time"!

May God bless our days and work!

Paper Trails People . . . Here, as we send out the last installment so far of *Paper Trails* . . . we can share more information with you about our present plans. Last time, if you remember, we spoke of our transition to Tanzania, in East Africa, to serve with the congregation of the Arusha Community Church. We now are planning to depart from Seattle a month from today on November 9, flying via Amsterdam, and scheduled to arrive at the Kilimanjaro Airport near Arusha on the next day. The congregation there have rented a newly constructed home for us to live in, and are concluding the process of getting our work permit and visa arrangements. We look forward to meeting more of them and engaging in an exciting ministry together!
We shall keep in touch with you via new reflections for the next *Paper Trails* volume. We understand there is no television over there, so some long evenings might be spent in spinning yarns about our new adventures . . . or even finishing *The Proclamation Project* . . . a book of sermons some of you so faithfully helped me transcribe via email while we were in La Paz, Bolivia. I don't want all your work to be in vain! Meanwhile, Dory and I will get back to packing, planning, and preparing to blast out of here the day after the election next month!
Following, to end this volume of *Paper Trails*, is our closing newsletter article to the church in Jakarta that says a lot we could say now!

Let Us Worship God

When we began our ministry with you here at the Jakarta Community Church, I made some remarks in a sermon that summoned us as we commenced our work together as pastor and people to "begin with the *Benediction.*" I noted that we needed to *open* our work together with God's blessing not just find that blessing as the *outcome* of those efforts. This church sings a marvelous benediction to each other at the close of worship, as we disperse to go our separate ways into our other worlds of work and home and family.

When the Apostle Paul wrote to the churches he usually began *and* ended with a word of blessing. Indeed, he sought God's blessing on his people every step of the way. "Grace to you all and Peace" can be paraphrased as "may you begin with God's favor, and therefore end with God's fullness." So we sought to begin our work here together with God's blessing.

Now, as we end this time together in our common ministry maybe we need to affirm the opposite truth . . . and finish with a *Call to Worship!* We began in grace and we conclude in peace, but in all of this we need to hear afresh the call of God to worship, witness and service.

The "chief end" or purpose of human life is to glorify and enjoy God forever, as the proper answer to the first question, of the *Westminster Shorter Catechism* put it. We need to keep that "chief end" in mind as we conclude our time together in ministry in this amazing and dynamic Indonesian capital city of Jakarta.

So now, may we hear this word also: "Let us worship God!" To begin with God's favor and end with God's fullness is to relate to the source and goal of all our blessing and work . . . the God who creates, redeems and sustains us, the One from whom we come and to whom we go, and whose worship is perfect freedom and joy indeed!

Jakarta is no stranger to the never-ending attractions, distractions, amusements, and demands of our confused world that summon us to a life of endless idolatry. The gods of self-fulfillment, career, economic success, reputation, family, national pride and trivial consumerism all too often get in the way of our vision of the one true God of all the earth. Forgetting who *God* is . . . we lose sight of who *we* are as well . . . and "where there is no vision the people perish."

Will we let God be God . . . and our church be the Church? And thus find our lives truly blessed with the grace which begins our work together, and the peace that concludes it?

An unknown writer in the Roman Empire in the first century of the Christian era wrote a description of *The Christians in the World.* In the famous *Letter to Diognetus* he seems filled with awe and admiration at how uniquely this new people live . . . and says of them, that "every foreign land is a homeland to them, and every homeland a foreign land, because their true Commonwealth is in heaven." This really came home to me again in a recent baptism, where Christian hands from Australia, Indonesia and America were laid on the head of a young man from Wales!

We have been richly blessed by our time in ministry with you these past eight months! We have done some wonderful things together, made some marvelous friends, and will never forget you! Truly, you have made us feel at home in a foreign land. Dory and I thank God for you, and wish you all the best in your life together as you are even now preparing to call a new pastor in the days to come. May our parting words to each other be . . .

"Go now in peace . . . never be afraid . . ." and . . . "Let us worship God!" Gratefully yours . . . in Christ!

—Jakarta Community Church Newsletter, May 2000.

Paper Trails—May 2007

Here begins anew my *Paper Trails* contributions to your idle moments or delete box. We left off sending these when leaving for Africa in November of 2005. Many of you since then have received our *Tanzania Tales*, written by both Dory and me, regarding our ministry and adventures in Arusha, Tanzania, and our subsequent visit to South Africa en route home. We had a wonderful year with the Arusha Community Church, made a lot of new friends and found opportunities for service and outreach that were most rewarding. Now, back home, after five months taking care of a lot of things here I feel the need to get back to sharing my reflections with whoever would like to read them. Some of you have inquired of me why there have been none recently. In any event they are being continued, in order to keep me off the streets and communicating. I realize that I have some I wanted to share and didn't get to it. Thanks for listening and we hope you welcome these next installments. To those of you who are new to our list we welcome you into this process of occasional words to break up your day! I will include selected excerpts from our *Tanzania Tales* and some previous ones from *The La Paz Papers* and *The 9/11 Papers* and others I didn't get out because of our transition to Africa. I begin with one of the "spy" stories! . . . added to my *Edinburgh Papers*.

Paper Trails #81

The Spy Who Had to . . . ?

Sometime around 1963, while a student in Edinburgh, returning to my room on the top floor of the New College Residence I found my German roommate Eberhardt trying to decipher a note in his hand. I inquired what he was up to, and he said he was reading a message given to him by an "old Scottish fellow" who often showed up at the German Congregation in Edinburgh to get a meal or some handouts to keep him going.

Eberhardt was serving the German Congregation in Edinburgh during the Pastor's absence and had befriended this man several times. Having won his confidence he now had this communication from him that he was trying to make sense of. Thinking I might be of some assistance, I offered to help and took a look at it. The note was written partly in English and partly in German. I read it carefully and soon became convinced that this piece of paper was from no ordinary destitute or homeless Scot.

The man's note began by asserting that he was born in Salzburg, Austria, and "began working for the 'der Fuehrer' in Aberdeen, Scotland in 1936." This immediately alerted me even further to the possibility that we had a very interesting note in our hands. He went on to assert some more details about himself that I can't quite remember now, and some of it was in German, but I do recall that his last words were "May the *Reich* rise again!"

"Eberhardt," I said, "this is no ordinary old Scottish tramp. They are not likely to write in German, nor keep in touch with a German congregation. Do you know anymore about him?" He said that for all he knew he was just a homeless or destitute Scottish man.

It occurred to me then who he might be . . . and I observed, "You know, Eberhardt, he just might be a Nazi spy who got stranded years ago when Germany lost the war." Eberhardt thought this was a foolish idea and asserted that he was just a silly old vagrant fellow.

"I don't think so," I said . . . And it seemed now obvious to me that this man, not being on the winning side in the conflict that was WWII . . . found himself without a country . . . so what else could he do but go into hiding? He certainly couldn't turn himself in to the British authorities and be arrested as an enemy spy, and he likewise would be unable to return home to a defeated nation.

This led me to reflect on how many other former "spies" there might be in the world who were not on the winning side in a conflict and had to spend the rest of their days hiding out in plain view and making their way through life as best as they could muster, seeking the help of whoever might be of a sympathetic mind and had the ability to assist them. What a sad, risky and fascinating tale they would have to tell, faced with spending the rest of their days leading a secret life long after it had been their vocation.

This, I thought, would make for a very interesting book.

Little did I know then that one of the best mystery tales ever written was being published at about that time . . . *The Spy Who Came in from the Cold* by John Le Carre. It tells the story of a British secret agent who defected to East Germany during the Cold War. The story became a classic and then a movie starring Richard Burton and made its author famous. I have yet to read it or see the film!

Some spies have to *stay out* in the cold. Maybe some people should write a book about it when it occurs to them!

Healing Wall

Something there is . . . that doesn't like a wall . . .

—Robert Frost

"The Wall"
Came to our town one day
With its 58,000 plus names of
Those who died in a war
That no one really wanted . . .

We gathered to commemorate
The visit of "The Wall" . . .
Remembering that
This was to be "A Wall that Heals" . . .
The Chaplain said such gracious words
We could have been at Gettysburg . . .
The Coast Guard choppers flew a "missing man formation" . . .
Wreathes were laid in solemn tribute.

But then it ended in the strangest way.
Men were playing games with guns . . .
Twirling them on their fingers,
And tossing them to each other as if playing catch
Or shooting baskets.

Men should not play this way with guns.
Not in this land . . . where guns are gods.
We shoot people in this jungle of a culture
That knows no battle lines,
And guns are everywhere
Waiting for people to pick them up
And kill each other . . . or themselves.
Because we are a nation addicted to guns.

But "it's only discipline" I'm told . . .
This playing with guns.
"And you wouldn't understand
Unless you'd been in the military . . .
Where you'd know the one thing
You need the most in war is discipline."

It's only a discipline I'm told . . .
But it is a discipline that leads to death.
Men should not play with guns this way . . .
They bring forth baby-faced boys
Who also like to play with guns,
And launch their Tet Offensives in the cafeteria,
Or turn schoolyards into My Lai's
Not so far from home.

It is deadly quiet
While these men spin and toss their guns
Then the audience applauds . . .
As if this were a fitting climax to honoring
Those who died from guns
When nobody was playing around.

All this took place on a sunny day in our town
In front of the replica of a Wall that has three times
The names our phone book has . . .
Names that cry out in silence
For us to stop this madness
Before it kills us all . . .
And someone has to build another Wall
To prove we didn't learn a thing . . .
Except that we're good at building walls
And shutting others in or out,
In a deadly game that is no game,
And refuses to find healing at "The Wall."

—from A Word in Season.

Saber Rattling

No End to War Not Good Start to the New Century

My wife and I were appalled and highly offended when President Bush announced the "war on terror" as "first war of the Twenty-first Century."

Could we not begin a new century with a better agenda than endless warfare?

Early in the last century, we had what came to be referred to as "the war to end all wars" in the carnage of World War I.

Now our president seems almost eager to start World War III.

One of the great World War I poets, Wilfred Owen, who died in the trenches in that mindless conflict, called for "the next war" when, as he said, "each proud fighter brags he wars on Death—for lives, not men—for flags."

Our bellicose (or should we say "bullicose") president seems hell-bent on starting a next war that will end all wars—and most likely, given his great imperial affection for our nuclear capacity—everything else as well.

When will we learn the ways of peace?

—Graham Hutchins, Port Angeles,
The Seattle Post Intelligencer, November 5, 2007.

The Gospel According to Scrooge

"It was the best of times; it was the worst of times."
—Charles Dickens, A *Tale of Two Cities*

These opening lines of one of Dickens great books could well be written of our own days on our blessed but troubled planet. Never have many had it so good . . . and never have so many had it so bad. Our world, so full of promise . . . is also threatened like never before. Maybe at this Christmastime we need to hear again some really good news . . . To begin my *Paper Trails* once more I will start with excerpts from a newsletter article written a few years back, called *The Gospel According to Scrooge!*

Old Scrooge has a bad reputation. Everyone knows him as the epitome of greed and selfishness in utter defiance of the human need around him. True enough, he is often portrayed powerfully, and is therefore easily remembered as a stingy old skinflint . . . a "Bah Humbug!" sort of a man. But this is really unfair to Ebenezer Scrooge! And to Charles Dickens who created him. We need to know the rest of his story.

It is a tale of transformation. Of "redemption" in the true biblical sense. The story of a changed heart and mind. Of a man who overnight turned around and went in another direction, and moved from greed to generosity, from selfishness to sharing, from living out his days as a sour old man to one with such new life in his bones that he wanted to skip and hop like a schoolboy. [How powerfully this was portrayed for us recently in our own production of *A Christmas Carol* by Jim Drennan, loaned to us, happily, from the First Christian Church. Masterfully he demonstrated how this old curmudgeon had a profound change of heart and had "become like a little child."] When Tiny Tim exclaimed, "God bless us everyone," he included Scrooge within the orbit of God's gracious provision. The crippled boy bore witness to how the deformed man had become as a little child. And the selfish old man provided a way to help Tiny Tim to grow into a mature adult.

The more I ponder *A Christmas Carol* the more impressed I am with this great work. Dickens weaves a veritable tapestry of meaning out of the simple cultural joys of Christmas and family life, the Gospel message, biting social commentary, and just plain good storytelling, to present us with an unforgettable summons to hear the good news and live a new life.

A friend of mine had a marvelous cardboard cutout of Scrooge in his most cantankerous demeanor . . . a mean old miser of a man, who nonetheless on his lapel wears a large metal button that says: *Joy to the World!* Scrooge certainly hadn't put on a "happy face"! It is a hilarious contrast! Joy to the world indeed!

But the real Scrooge of Dickens's tale didn't just put on an outward appearance of the meaning of the season. He was totally transformed and even his face as well as his deeds showed it! The story ends with the word that no one could " 'keep Christmas' like Ebenezer Scrooge, who kept it henceforth all the year."

In this season of Advent, may we too discern the spirits of our past, present and future in the light of God's gift to us of time and grace, and awaken us with Scrooge to the true meaning of Christmas and how joy *really* comes to the world!

Thank you Geri Schmitt, for directing this production and leading us through this wonderful story again! It is both a timeless message and a very timely tale. In our modern world where greed is "in," and our society is rapidly developing a new hatred for the poor, we need to hear again and again the Gospel according to Scrooge! And to discover as he did, that we can have a new heart and a new spirit by the grace of God. Merry Christmas everyone!

—from "The View from the Tower," The Tower Echoes, First UMC, Port Angeles, 1996.

PS. Our Twenty-first-Century world today . . . confronted with terrorism, global warming, genocide and famine, an impending recession, and the malaise of despair and selfishness, needs to hear this word afresh . . . and discover how to be transformed anew to celebrate the Good News of Christmas all the year.

The 9/11 Papers VI

Revised for the Port Angeles Rotary, 12-18-2002

Christmas Incognito

We received an email from Indonesia this week that was a response to some reflections I wrote a year ago at Christmas regarding the events that had overtaken the world at that time. I was asked to read one of my Christmas poems for this occasion, but would rather share the following adapted for today from my *9/11 Papers* I wrote then.

We are into the celebration of Christmas. We want to celebrate with joy and merriment. And yet we are aware—all too aware—that it is a rather somber world these days. Christmas can't even really be an escape from some of the reality that impinges on our consciousness. We are not only into a new century but into one that looks disturbingly like the last one, and might even be worse. And we all know that to a great extent this is the result of the terrorist acts of 9/11. So what does the message of this season of Christmas have to do with the horrible events that on that fateful day brought a sense of outrage, dread and sorrow, of uncertainty and crisis to the world?

There are some interesting and even perverse parallels here . . . what some might call "parables of contrast."

Christmas is the great feast or celebration of the Incarnation . . . of *the Word made Flesh* . . . "Bone of our bone and flesh of our flesh" . . . of God coming among us and hiding in our humanity. The claim is made that the Son of God was born as a human baby—not in the citadels of power or wealth or influence—but in a cattle stall to a peasant family far from home. A real birth . . . very real . . . and not even noticed, except for a few shepherds. The Son of God—incognito—yet "hiding out in full public view."

Incognito means "hiding out in full public view." This phrase is one used of the terrorists of September 11th! They were among us as those who were "hiding out in full public view." Somebody's neighbors, maybe on your street or mine—shopping at Wal-Mart, renting cars, looking like us, learning to fly, eating in restaurants, booking tickets on the airlines, catching the ferry from Victoria. Trying, and mostly succeeding to be—unnoticed, unrecognized, unobtrusive—until their dread mission was accomplished.

There have been reports that some 20-30,000 terrorists—trained in the al-Qaida camps in Afghanistan or elsewhere since 1996—are all over the world—"hiding out in full public view." We cannot call out the Marines to find these people. They too could be your neighbors or mine—eating in our restaurants, shopping at our grocery stores—looking a lot like us—waiting for some signal to carry out another dreadful mission.

This is a warning we are all aware of now—but it might also be a parable. I don't mean here to spoil Christmas for you today. But to relate it to the reality we all have to deal with.

Soren Kierkegaard has an essay . . . *On the "man of faith" and the "man of infinite resignation."* I remember reading it years ago . . . and discovering the great surprise in it . . . that these two men look exactly alike! They are worlds apart—but to all outward appearances look just like each other! One has faith—or confidence in God; the other in blind fate or some manifest destiny. So it is today. We have been attacked by those who have blended into our culture and common life and claim to be "men of faith"—but, who, having hijacked our planes and their own religion, are really men of "infinite resignation." Which are we?

The impact of the unfolding disclosure that Christmas celebrates—the manifestation and demonstration of the reality of who Christ is—as God hiding out in full public view in our humanity in order to save us—is a momentous event in the history of the world. God is so hidden in our midst that his Son is born as a Hebrew baby in a stable and dies as a criminal on Roman cross—this is what some have called the "ultimate pseudonym of God." Talk about "incognito!" Yet when the significance of this was realized it finally split history into before and after. Do we who are in the "after"—have a bit of amnesia—perhaps? Has Christmas been turned, as it was last year, into a save the economy from the terrorists shopping season instead of the disclosure and discovery of *Emmanuel*—"God with us?"

The Christmas season really begins on Christmas Day and lasts for twelve days . . . the next day is the Feast of the Epiphany . . . often called the Eastern Christmas . . . when the Eastern Orthodox churches celebrate the birth of Christ. Epiphany means "manifestation" or disclosure, or a revealing of that which had been among us but not noticed.

September 11, 2001 was an "epiphany" of sorts—a "manifestation" or a revealing of that which had been among us for some time. Now we know, but then we did not recognize or refused to notice. On 9/11/01 it was demonstrated—became clear in some terrible ways—that we had then—and may still now have among us those whose purpose is not to save us but to destroy us. Those who came among us then came to bring terror and death to the world. The One who came among us whose birthday we celebrate this season came to bring "Joy to the World."

Does this season of the year make us aware again of the One who came to be "God with us" . . . or is it now just an odd cultural event that is "nice" and a good time for us to be together in these dark days? Do we need to further realize the fullness of meaning that resides in the disclosures of our faith?

Are we a people of faith, or a people of infinite resignation? Are we more impressed with power—or with truth? Is our confidence in the God who has come to save all people—or a God who seeks to destroy some? Some things to think about . . . in this year of our Lord . . . 2002.

Port Angeles Papers

God's Great "Nevertheless"!

A distinguished French Calvinist theologian once observed that "the key to the Old Testament is the word 'nevertheless.' " He was thinking, says J.S. Whale, of the great "two beat rhythm" of justice and mercy, law and grace, in those awesome books of ancient Israel, where God confronts us with: "forgiveness through judgment, love through wrath, gospel through law . . . God's 'proper work' is made effective through his 'alien work,' which means redemption through enslavement, homecoming through exile, renewal through destruction, resurrection through death." Thus the story of the people of God is one of deliverance to, through, and from disaster . . . again and again. But in and through it all, this God is nevertheless . . . with them, and wills to be their God. In a phrase I've often quoted at gravesides, the Psalmist, confessing an experience of bitterness and rebellion toward God, suddenly asserts:

"Nevertheless I am continually with you,
you hold me by my right hand,
You guide me with your counsel,
and afterward you will receive me to glory."

—Psalms 73:23-24.

Maybe this is how we can sum up what Easter means . . . it is God's great "Nevertheless" to us! It is God's amazing intrusion of the unexpected. It is the surprise of the ages that suddenly dawns on you as the surprise of your life! It is the discovery of the truth of Jesus's word to the disciples as he went to the Cross . . . "In the world you have tribulation, but be of good cheer, I have overcome the world."

Easter is a cry on the lips of a defeated people, who nevertheless can say with St. Paul . . . "Thanks be to God who *gives* us the victory through our Lord Jesus Christ! It is the experience of multitudes of men and women . . . who, finding themselves in the valley of death's shadow, suddenly fear no evil because they discover One is with them . . . who has been there before.

Easter is a new hearing by an old and tired world of an astounding breakthrough from beyond with a voice that cries . . . "Behold, I am making all things new!" It is God's great Nevertheless to a world that had concluded: "It's all over." It is the discovery that the long awaited "End of the world" is really a *"Now* is the day of salvation!" Easter is the joy of knowing that even though we have acted unworthy of God and our calling as God's people . . . we can affirm "nevertheless" with the Psalmist that we are "continually" with the One who wills to be with us in caring love and restoring grace, and who will ultimately lead us to glory. Easter is God's reconciling word to our rebellious acts . . . God's triumphant "Yes!" to death's defiant "No!" God's word not merely of comfort or of hope . . . but of Victory over all that would leave the world a place of grief and graves.

As God's great "Nevertheless to us . . . it is God's great Amen to Life!" A Joyous Easter to you all!

—from "A View from the Tower," *Tower Echoes*, Easter 1999.

An Amazing Trip to Tiahuanaco and the Past

We have finally made it out of town again for a couple of short trips. For several weeks now the *campesinos* have blocked a lot of highways with rocks and prevented travel to the Yungas [the valleys below the Altiplano enroute the lowlands and jungles of Bolivia] and on the Altiplano and the routes to Lake Titicaca and Peru. The *campesinos* are demonstrating in order to win a list of concessions from the Government regarding betterment of their lives and working conditions, and also on behalf of teachers, small businessmen and vendors and transportation workers including the truckers that take their produce to market. Many of them work in agriculture and produce some of the best food anywhere. Some of them work in coca production which was a staple of their lives here for generations before Norte Americano's [that's us in the USA mostly] came up with the chemical means to turn it into cocaine. We are spending millions of dollars to help the government here eradicate the coca fields, in the naïve assumption that this would stop the drug traffic in America. The effort is failing and many of the *campesinos* need a way to make a living producing other crops, etc. or have alternative industries that will support their families. So they demonstrate, usually quite peacefully, but with some frustrating interruption of normal life in this republic.

Anyway, a few days ago [July 11] we paid a visit to Tiahuanaco, the site of an ancient civilization in the Andes that was a forerunner of the famous Inca civilization that came much later. It was astonishing for us to read about it in our new *Footprints Bolivia Handbook* purchased in Port Angeles just before we left for our assignment down here. It is tempting just to type out the amazing material in the handbook in order to share this incredible information with you. So why not? Here goes; read this!

Archeologists had long believed that Tiahuanaco was a relatively unimportant era in the history of Andean civilization. Until, that is, Alan Kolata, an anthropologist from the University of Illinois in Chicago, led an archeological expedition to the site in 1986. Kolata came up with some amazing finds, not least of which was evidence that the Pampa Koani, now barely able to sustain a population of 7,000 in dire poverty, was, 1,500 years ago a vast agricultural area that produced enough to support 125,000 people.

Kolata's expedition showed that the Pampa Koani was just one Lake Titicaca Valley among many that produced great harvests every year for 1,000 years. This was due to an immense system of raised fields built by the Tiahuanaco Empire more than 2,000 years ago. These harvests fed the equivalent of the entire population of Bolivia today and even allowed for surpluses to be stored for poor years. The raised fields proved that, far from being a minor period in Andean civilization, Tiahuanaco was a great imperial capital and the inspiration for the better known Inca Empire that followed it.

The Tiahuanaco Empire comprised nearly half of present-day Bolivia, southern parts of Peru, the northwest section of Argentina and nearly half of Chile. It was built on the vast produce of its agricultural systems.

Of all the accomplishments of the Tiahuanaco culture, including its trade routes, architecture and artistry, the single greatest feat has to be its system of raised fields. The many, many years of empirical study that went into perfecting them, the sheer effort of building them and the amazing levels of production that came out of them are all unparalleled in history, according to U.S. anthropologist Alan Kolata.

The ancient people of Tiahuanaco had to overcome the many problems that bedevil local farmers today—floods, droughts, soil exhaustion and salinization from Lake Titicaca's slightly salty waters. Even international aid agencies have failed to improve conditions. At such extreme altitude the climate seems too harsh and the soil too poor to succeed in making a difference.

The system of raised fields developed by the Tiahuanaco people was so carefully engineered and built that many of them remain intact today. They are massive constructions, over one meter high, with planting surfaces sometimes as large as fifteen meters wide [approximately forty-five feet] and two hundred meters long. Each is a carefully layered structure with a thick cobblestone base which is covered with a layer of impermeable clay. Over the clay is a layer of coarse gravel, and then a layer of finer gravel. Over all that sits the topsoil.

The raised fields lie parallel to one another, separated by deep irrigation channels running in straight lines or graceful curves which form precise geometric patterns. The irrigation ditches provided water in times of drought and the elevated fields protected crops in times of flooding. These fields and ditches cover over fifty square kilometers of the Pampa Koani. To achieve this, the ancient engineers straightened the Catari River and moved it 1,500 meters [approximately 4,500 feet] to the east.

The layer of clay at the base of the fields prevented the brackish water of nearby Lake Titicaca from seeping up from below ground and into the topsoil. The exact positioning of the fields and ditches was designed to take advantage of the fierce Andean sun. By efficiently exposing the ditches to the sun, the water in them gets enough heat by day to protect the fields from frost damage during the bitterly cold nights [at 13-14,000 feet]. The heated water in the ditches also promoted the rapid growth of algae that fed the fish. Furthermore, it attracted a resident population of ducks which also entered the local diet as meat and eggs. Duck droppings, decayed algae and fish remains then formed a rich sludge that was scraped off the bottom of the ditches to be used as fertilizer for the topsoil.

The idea of using this ancient, long forgotten agricultural technology to increase output on the barren Altiplano is currently under discussion, spurred on by the efforts of Alan Kolata. If the Tiahuanaco people could grow what they needed to eat and more, using the same fields and without the benefit of tractors, water pumps and chemical fertilizers, surely it could be done again. Rural Bolivians today could yet reap what their ancestors sowed.

—*Footprint Bolivia Handbook*, 2nd Edition, pp. 109-110. Copyright Footprint Handbooks Ltd., 2000, Bath, England.

This is just incredible! . . . Even wound up as an illustration in a sermon on . . . *The People of a Promising Past—The Way of Memory*! "Ask for the ancient paths, where the good way is, and walk in it." Jeremiah 6:6!

Sent: Wednesday, September 26, 2001 11:45 P.M.
The 9/11 Papers

Doubt in the Barbershop

I went to get a haircut the other day. While I was waiting a man came into the barbershop and sat near me and began to read the paper. He was dressed rather formally in a dark suit and tie and shiny black shoes that almost looked like a uniform. He didn't even appear like he needed a haircut, but was already finely trimmed in his mustache and short cropped hair. He was of a swarthy complexion and looked like a stranger in town . . . Maybe of Mediterranean or even Middle Eastern background. I watched him some more as my hair was being cut . . . and in the impact of recent events could not help but wonder who he was. A hint of suspicion even began to grow in my mind. No one, anywhere, is safe anymore from the possible threat of strange people who might be hiding out even in barbershops. Is not this the city where a terrorist was apprehended getting off the ferry from Victoria nearly two years ago? Did we learn anything from that? After the events of 9-11 . . . we can't help but think about such things again. Who is this man sitting there waiting for a haircut he doesn't even need? . . . and so I reflected on the wider context of these days and the immediate context of the barbershop.

The barber finally finished with me . . . and as I was paying him, the man rose from his chair and took off his jacket to get his own hair cut, and it was then I saw the epaulets on the shoulders of his shirt and the unmistakable symbols of THE SALVATION ARMY.

I was too embarrassed even to apologize.

A Flight into Fear . . . late September 2001

One of our many friends at the church retreat on the shores of Puget Sound took us to catch the Kitsap Transit van to the Seattle-Tacoma airport . . . It took the van nearly twenty minutes waiting in a long line after arriving there to access the drop off point for the passengers catching departing flights. Such was a first sign to us of the cautions that have been implemented since the tragic events of September 11. Except of course for the subdued and sometimes somber mood of everyone either on the bus or in the various pick up points along the way.

Our flight left Seattle on time at around 10:30 . . . A "red-eye" all-night flight to Philadelphia . . . a kind of welcome destination in a way . . . as its name implies the love that should prevail among brothers. I also noted how ironic it is in a world so filled with signs of hatred.

We arrived having slept a good deal and then seeing the lights of many cities large and small as we traveled east across this incredible but troubled land of America. All those lights and cities on this beautiful night with clear skies and even a friendly moon seemed somehow comforting. Even better, the dawn was breaking over Philadelphia and we saw the city emerging from the dark night into the light of day that glistened on the river and the windows of buildings, and we landed easily and a little ahead of schedule at about 6:20 A.M.

We found our transfer gate and even got some coffee and a cinnamon roll to wake us up while waiting for our flight to Bangor, Maine. We felt rather good about having flown again in spite of the climate of fear that gripped the nation and made many cancel their travel plans accordingly. We had flown so much just a month ago in South America . . . but noticed not only in others but also ourselves some real hesitation about getting again into what seemed now the not so "friendly skies."

We purchased the *Philadelphia Inquirer* and read the various articles that interested and informed us . . . and there were many . . . as that paper like others sought ways to deal with this new situation of fear and courage, resolve and hesitation that characterizes our nation at this time.

Our flight to Bangor was called and we lined up with our IDs and boarding passes to finish our journey to the East where my sister and brother-in-law were to meet us. We boarded a smaller plane this time, not like the Boeing 757 that had carried us from Seattle, but a twin engine turbo-prop that was more than adequate for the only six passengers it was to take to Bangor. We were scheduled to arrive in Bangor, Maine, at 9:59.

We fastened our seat belts as the engines were starting . . . and then . . . the pilot suddenly pointed out that the right engine was failing to function properly and we would have to delay until a mechanic could come out and check it. So . . . back to the papers again . . . and some watching of the mechanic as he climbed up to fix the problem. Again the call to fasten seat belts . . . and prepare for departure when the pilot announced that now there were problems with the other engine, and it was best if we deplaned this time and wait for an announcement to board again or make other arrangements. So we returned to the departure lounge . . . which brought to mind Auden's lines about "the airports almost deserted." About a half hour later we were told the flight was canceled and we would have to reschedule. I called my brother-in-law in Maine and happily discovered they had not left Bar Harbor for Bangor to pick us up but had been checking with the airline and seemed to know more about it than we did! We then found that another flight was leaving at 1:15 and we could get seats on it. More newspaper articles and some good naps . . . more waiting and then some lunch at a Japanese food counter and finally the flight was called and we boarded again.

Here . . . the six from the morning flight joined those who were scheduled to take this one making about eighteen passengers in all. We were assigned seats in the very back of the plane and fastened our seat belts and prepared to finally depart Philadelphia.

All seemed well . . . but then I noticed a man who looked like he might be from the Middle East sitting a few rows ahead of us. The flight attendant came by and told him he must put his large duffel bag into an overhead compartment. He complied and was able to stuff it into one after removing some shoes from it. I felt somewhat relieved at his hearty smile and jovial bantering with the flight attendant and his very American accent.

The pilot then announced that there was some trouble getting the right engine started and we needed to wait a few minutes while a mechanic was called to check out and perhaps fix the problem. So we waited . . . again . . . and even exchanged some conversation with some of the passengers around us. I even told of misreading, in this climate of suspicion, the appearance of what turned out to be a Salvation Army officer while getting a haircut the other day.

The mechanics did their work again . . . on the right engine generator . . . again . . . of this plane that was exactly like the one we had boarded a few hours ago. We prepared once more for takeoff, and suddenly the man we had registered a bit of concern about in our minds signaled to the flight attendant he needed to go to the restroom. She seemed to indicate he could and he got up, took something out of his bag in the compartment above and then came back to the rear of the plane and entered the restroom. He was there quite awhile, and I for one began to wonder what was going on. I chastised myself for being somewhat suspicious of all of this . . . yet noted in my mind that this is very unusual. The rest rooms are off limits on the ground as we have heard announced many times before. And especially this would be the case as a plane is about to take off. The flight attendant was already strapped into her seat up front when the man came out of the rest room behind the galley. We had even begun to wonder if she remembered he was in there.

We taxied to the runway . . . ready again to depart. Suddenly the pilot announced that we had problems with other engine . . . and we must return and deplane until this too was attended to by the mechanics. Was this the same plane? It certainly had the same problems . . . And it seems we had heard all of this before. So . . . we returned to the loading dock and deplaned again, and were told to wait near the departure gate until announcement of the disposition of this flight. This we did . . . except for the man who some of us were watching. He reappeared later when the flight was canceled to get in line with the rest of us to make other arrangements. I stood near him and heard him say he needed to get back to work. I asked him if there were any other airlines flying in and out of Bangor, Maine. He replied that he did not know. A moment later I ventured to ask . . . "What is your work?" "We run a Pakistani restaurant," he replied. More conversations elicited the information that he was returning from Florida where he had been on vacation. Meanwhile another man in the line was angry because he maintained that this had been the same plane we had been on for the morning flight and it should have been taken out of service and repaired.

We suddenly decided we might be able to rebook and fly into Bar Harbor instead of Bangor and to our surprise found it possible, by way of Boston and so we left a couple hours late. At Logan Airport in Boston, the *Boston Globe* headlines seem to scream at us in big red letters "LOGAN LAPSES . . ." The manager of the airport had been fired because of the lax security, as two of the hijacked planes had departed from there on that terrible Tuesday. The security was now in full force. There were U.S. Marshals, National Guard troops and State Police checking everything. For the third time that day this laptop computer had to be removed from its case and booted up and inspected.

What is going on here? . . . What made us suspicious of a jovial guy returning from a vacation in Florida in his shorts and sandals? And yet, he was one whose looks and actions began to raise some questions in our minds? We felt embarrassed at being perhaps a bit more prejudiced than we liked to think we are.

Or should we be so concerned? Perhaps we should. Will lives be lost in this land because people were too polite to ask questions? Did that flight attendant know something we didn't? Perhaps she knew this man from previous flights? Maybe she too was suspicious of his behavior ant alerted the captain to abort the flight? We will never know the answer to these questions.

Where is the fine line between a courage that surrenders neither to timidity or cowardice on the one hand or recklessness and foolhardiness on the other? Is it sometimes true that "conscience does make cowards of us all?" We are going to have to be careful . . . full of care . . . and caring . . . if we are going to function with some semblance of what used to be normal in this society. We need caution *and* tolerance. We need not surrender to fear *or* to hasty judgments, but must decide in every situation what course of action is indicated. It is interesting that much of what was going through my head was also occupying my wife's attention and concern. And I am sure it was on the minds of others. Perhaps they, like we, didn't mind at all that the afternoon flight to Bangor was canceled like the morning one.

We finally arrived at my sister's home in Bar Harbor. My brother-in-law checked the Bangor phone book and found more than a few ethnic restaurants listed but noted that there are no Pakistani restaurants in the Bangor area. Be careful . . . And travel well.

As I write this, a cartoon appeared this morning in the *Boston Globe* that indicates that many in our land, as I surmised, share the thoughts all of this elicited in my mind. It shows a man who had just boarded a plane and sees several of the passengers who were already seated ahead of him. He has a fearful grimace on his face, as he can't help but notice two Middle Eastern looking passengers and another whose headgear and dress indicate he is obviously a Muslim cleric. The caption above the picture reads: "This is a Test of America's Emergency Tolerance System."

Out to Africa!

We are taking this means to communicate with those of you in the congregation who may not have heard . . . we're still finding friends who didn't know about our going to live in East Africa for a year or so.

We have been invited to go to Arusha, Tanzania, to work with the Arusha Community Church, an English-speaking congregation, similar to the ones we served in Indonesia and Bolivia.

We are excited about working with this congregation of missionaries, medical practitioners, educators, UN Personnel, international service organization workers, business people and their families. They have an active program to minister to the many needs of the region; over half their budget is committed to this work. They have also built a beautiful and functional building and are participating in construction of a new hospital next to the church.

Their church council is in the process of helping us secure a visa since we will be working in the country. Though this is a position without salary they are providing the expenses of our ministry with them, a furnished house, transportation and ways of meeting other needs as we all identify them.

Arusha is about a mile above sea level, in a temperate climate, where coffee and bananas and other fruits and vegetables are grown. It is also the place from which many safaris go into the Serengeti and climbers come to ascend nearby Mt. Kilimanjaro, the highest mountain in Africa.

We are certainly going to miss our friends in this congregation and community and all the good times we have in this beautiful part of the world, but time will go fast and we will return to engage in ministry with you here again. We will be sending reports about our life and work there, with impressions and stories from time to time.

We ask for your prayers and best wishes for our task of mission there, and should you plan a trip to Africa come stay at the Hutchins house . . . and bring chocolate chips! We hope to see and bid you good-bye before we leave on November 9 when we will say . . . *Kwa heri!* (good-bye in Swahili, the language of Tanzania).

Tanzanian Tales—Some glimpses of life in this amazing place . . .

Of the Moon, Human Need, Economics, Conversations . . .

Greetings from Tanzania . . . *Jambo!* . . . [Hello] . . . *Hujambo* . . . [you have nothing the matter?] . . . *Sijambo!* . . . [I have NOTHING the matter!] This is the way people greet each other in Kiswahili, the official language of Tanzania.

Moon Struck

The moon shines so brightly here, as do the stars . . . that it is astonishing to see. If we were near the sea down by Dar es Salaam or in Zanzibar, we might notice that the tides must be dancing to the powerful attraction of the orbiting moon and its romantic light. This reminds me that it has been well said, "A rising tide lifts all boats." But this phrase is usually expressed in reference to economic conditions in a particular place. Here in Africa it will take a pretty big economic tide to lift people out of the quicksands of poverty. Here in Tanzania the greatest income is from tourism. The only commodity on the world exchanges this country is noted for is beeswax. Tanzania is the world leader in beeswax! Probably a better, if less lucrative, reputation to have than the sale of armaments. That leadership role is left to us Americans. There are efforts to raise the economic tides here in Africa. Many seem to make matters worse. Even the discovery of oil in a few countries, not yet in Tanzania, is often transmogrified into corruption and greed and the rise of economic or military dictatorships.

There are some signs of hope. The new president in Liberia, a woman who was persecuted by former war lords has been elected no less, after a long period of civil war. She is a devout United Methodist Christian. Trade in Tanzania with South Africa has increased since the abolition of apartheid in that country, and this to the benefit of both people's.

This is a continent of amazing people. I think of an Anglican Bishop named Tutu, a Dutch Reformed President named de Klerk and a Methodist leader of an oppressed people named Mandela, who, in their battle against apartheid, all won the Nobel Prize for Peace in South Africa. Likewise, this is a continent of beautiful people. We have met people with names like Innocent, Immaculate, Patience, Peace, Faith and Emmanuel; and here in Tanzania their smiles are as bright as the moon . . . almost as if they are happily waiting for the tide to rise . . . and lift the boats of their lives toward the stars . . . this is Africa . . .

Impala Impressions

We had gone early to the Impala Hotel to have some supper before Graham attended a Rotary Meeting. We were seated in a pleasant cafe area near the swimming pool, and found ourselves in close proximity to two women at a table who were soon joined by a very well-dressed African man. It soon became clear from bits of conversation overheard that they were involved with the International Tribunal for Rwanda that meets here at the Arusha International Conference Center. This major UN presence in Arusha has caused the city to be referred to as the "Geneva of Africa." A number of people here with the UN worship with our congregation. From what we happened to overhear, one woman might have been a judge there, and the other was from New York and also an attorney and in Africa a few days before returning home and moving to Paris. The man, we believe, was from Kigali, in Rwanda, and there consulting with them on procedures and costs involved with incarcerating prisoners. We were somewhat surprised to be listening to a not altogether unpleasant conversation about the consequences of genocide. This too, is Africa. This too, is our world.

I accompanied Graham to the Rotary meeting where we heard a presentation requesting funds for the rebuilding and expansion of a Lutheran teaching hospital near Moshi that has been there for 105 years. Like the new Selian Hospital next to our church, this one too, is expanding to meet the rising need of a growing population. The Lutheran missionary presenting, with an African physician, observed that "Every man needs two women in his life, a wife to tell him what to do, and a secretary to do it." Graham introduced me as worth a wife and three secretaries, and so at the end of the meeting the president of the club picked me to draw the winner of the raffle . . . who turned out to be the British man next to us! An older man sitting near us of Indian descent with a white turban got up to say that he was in that hospital with a stroke that paralyzed his whole side in 1974 and was forever grateful for the care and skill that nursed him back to health again, and wholeheartedly endorsed the project. He sat down and turned to us and explained more, and then said, "Thank God!" This too, is Africa . . . and our world.

Serengeti Stranger

Dory went down to a nearby hardware store to pick up something, when a man came up and said he had seen her driving downtown the day before, recognized her and wanted to ask for some help. After talking, she told him to wait there and came home to get me and we returned to speak with him. He is very articulate in English and showed us a letter from a safari lodge in the Serengeti which summoned him for a job interview, and he needed the bus fare to get there. He presented us documentation that showed us he possessed very good skills and experience and explained that the lodge would not advance funds for interviews. We loaned him some money for the fare and dropped him off at the bus station. Several days later he returned to see us at our home and was elated. Though he had to stand up on the bus for over three hours, as far as Ngorongoro Crater, he finally arrived and had been offered the job. He returned to Arusha with a safari vehicle and was preparing to leave his wife for a month with their small children while he went back to work. He showed us a copy of the contract he had signed and wrote a request for funds from our church which he would repay when he returned from his work in early February. We prepared to take him home, when the guard at our compound noticed we had a low tire. Our new friend, nicely dressed and excited about his new lease on life showed us a place along the way to get our tire fixed and balanced . . . [it had a nail in it]. Then, as it was getting dark, we dropped him off nearby to catch a *dalla dalla* [busses . . . really vans . . . we will tell you about later]. We wished him well and went our separate ways. A few nights ago, we had a call from him in the Serengeti and he reminded us he would be back in a couple of weeks.

Sharing this story with some others . . . We were informed that he is one of the brightest con-artists in town, dresses well, speaks and writes eloquent English and should not be trusted. We will see. We hope we will not be disappointed. This too is Africa . . . and the world.

Discovering Iqwans

It was a tiny little store. We were referred to it by a parishioner who has lived here most of her life. She told us how to find it but we drove by it twice and even after a hand drawn map was provided we still had to park and go looking for it on foot. Many shops here have no sign identifying them and this one was in that category. Upon entry, we found a small room so well stocked you can find most anything in it. As such, it competes even with the rather new supermarket known as ShopRite and one or two others in Arusha . . . but with better prices.

We wandered around its few aisles of merchandise looking for what we needed on our list that was growing longer day by day. We found a great deal—even a lot of items—not even on our list! Everything from cocoa to capers, from candles to bay leaves and from Ziploc bags to Nutrella, a marvelous spread that is a blend of hazelnuts and chocolate that we haven't seen since Jakarta! We filled our grocery cart full to overflowing! Then we watched as some men put it all on a counter and one began writing down by hand everything we were purchasing. He filled three pages and then began totaling it up, with a sum at the end of each page. He then handed it to me to take it to the proprietor behind a sign that said "Pay Here," and he totaled it up again.

Meanwhile, another man began to put it all in a box and tied it with string. I pulled out my wallet to pay after the final total. It came to 82,500 Tanzanian shillings [about $75] . . . when I discovered I only had 78,000 shillings. The proprietor, a gentle Muslim man said, "That's alright, you can pay the rest next time," . . . to a brand new customer! Astonished, I was thinking what we could eliminate [like the Cadbury's Chocolate Bar I added to the cart while Dory went to get the car!] I said, well, maybe my wife has some cash left in her wallet. Sure enough, a minute later, when she showed up we had enough to cover the bill.

Tanzanian Tales

Advent in Arusha

The second Sunday here and Graham was in the pulpit again, much to his delight and mine and our new friends in the congregation's pleasure, to hear him deliver the Word so inspiringly and eloquently. Africa has been too good to us! That same Sunday though, after church, Graham broke his glasses fastening his seat belt! We went to Sunbeam Optical Centre and new lenses were ordered out of Nairobi, Kenya, for $200 and two weeks later he is happy with his "new" glasses.

Confirmation Celebration

Last Sunday we had an impressive service of Baptism and Confirmation. A tiny girl named Salamawit [the peaceful one] was baptized and her older cousin Sara confirmed. This was followed by Holy Communion and a celebration at the refreshment time. Then, a couple of hours later we went down yet another challenging dirt road, full of holes, ridges and rocks to the home of Dr. Mark and Mary Bura. We gathered with dozens of family and friends under a striped tent decorated with balloons and shining twists of tinsel. Sara the confirmand was the honoree on the entry patio with two great grandmothers, a great-great grandmother of ninety to ninety-five years [they are not certain of her age], her parents and a Tanzanian pastor and his wife beside him. The celebration began with introductions. Everyone is important, and literally everyone, young and old, large and small, gets introduced, no matter how long it takes. John Kraft, our architect friend, explained this in a very revealing way. He pointed out that in Copenhagen, for example . . . in the great public square there, the benches all face away from each other so people can enjoy their privacy, as we Westerners like to do. But in East Africa, the benches in public places face each other so people can gather around and talk. It comes from the nomadic life of the Maasai where everyone counted, consensus was sought, and all needed to be together to survive.

Mma Bura's [Mma is a Swahili term of respect used for all women] sisters were there in traditional Tanzanian dress, gleefully applauding and using traditional tongue clicking as a sign of approval. After all were well fed it was time for *Ngoma*, dancing, singing and drumming [in this case on a five-gallon plastic container], with women from senior citizens to a small girl of about four with her mother's scarf wrapped around her, bending over and happily swinging to and fro and soon joined by a teenage boy, who challenged Sara to see who could outdo the other in an exuberant dance of life.

From Laughter to Tears

As the mist from Olodonyo Orok [Maasai for black mountain/Mt. Meru] surrounds us we write both of death and grief and life and love. The other evening, soon after the sun had set, warming the earth with its glow of reds and orange, a knock at our door summoned and Graham called, "who's there?" A muffled, hardly audible voice, sobbed, "Kristine." As the door opened Dory heard the cries and ran down the stairs to find our young neighbor, a teacher at the International School overcome with grief. She had just heard that one of her pre-school students, a four-year-old boy, Toby, had died. We talked into the night, seeking to console her and help her deal with facing her eleven remaining students the next day.

On Monday morning we met at our house with John Kraft, our Council Chair, and Father Pat Patten, a priest, and with our musician Linda Jacobson to plan a memorial service at ACC for Tuesday afternoon. Little Toby who died suddenly of cerebral malaria, had only been here for six months. The family comes from New Jersey and Toby and his older brother Luke came here with his parents who are on sabbatical from Rutgers University. Toby's mother Dorothy Schroeder has spent over twenty years in East Africa doing research as an anthropologist among the Maasai, especially on the role of women in their response to the missionary impact upon their people. Father Patten, a friend of Dorothy's for years, is a pilot who runs his medical flying service all over the greater Arusha area. John Kraft is an architect and a graduate of Notre Dame with the heart of a priest. We met for several hours around our dining room table, planning the service. We all then visited the family of little Toby and prepared together to celebrate his life. The day Toby died the medical service had evacuated a woman who suffered a snakebite, another woman had twins, and lost her life unable to get to help in time, though the twins survived, and another woman was airlifted out of a village with several compound fractures. Then the call came of the tragedy of Toby's passing, and Father Patten flew again, this time in the middle of the night to Nairobi to pick up Toby's mother who was there doing research and to meet her parents who had come from America to visit. They arrived to the news of the tragic loss of their grandson.

The service was full of mourners to help share the grief of this loss. Graham presided, John welcomed and informed the congregation, Father Pat preached a powerful sermon, a friend and church member read the lesson, others did a responsive psalm, and Toby's parents Rick and Dorothy, and his brother Luke shared some poignant and humorous accounts of his brief life and times with us. About fifty kids from the school sang his favorite song, "Jingle Bells." His teacher, our neighbor Kristine, and her principal presented a beautiful Zanzibar chest to the family, filled with pictures of and by Toby and his friends. Linda both played and arranged music, including a string ensemble, and a Maasai women's choir to sing the Lord's Prayer in their language during the service. They stayed and sang more Maasai songs at the fellowship time afterwards. Toby was the fourth young ex-pat child to die here in five months. One was hit by a train, one died in a motorcycle accident, another was attacked by a leopard, and Toby died of malaria, though his parents had taken every precaution to protect him from it. In fact, the very preventive medicine he was on . . . Maalaron . . . is one of the best anti-malaria medicines available, but it actually masked his symptoms until it was too late. In all of Africa, one child dies every five minutes of malaria. Much of this could be prevented for less than a $5 investment in mosquito netting, according to Dr. Mark Jacobson.

We designed the service to express the longing for light, peace and comfort appropriate for the occasion, and also for the Advent season. We found the great Advent hymn *"O Come, O Come Emmanuel"* expressed it very well . . . we used the first verse from it as an antiphon for the readings from Psalm 139 and at the end we sang several verses with the refrain added. It was powerful . . . Lines like:

that mourns in lonely exile here . . .
and
disperse the gloomy clouds of night,
and death's dark shadows put to flight . . .

seemed so appropriate for both the sorrow felt by the whole community and the longing of Advent in a time of such drastic need not only in this setting but in the world today. Sad as it may seem . . . this could well be our theme as we greet you before the holidays . . . and express a fervent hope for our world, that we might discover new life in honor of the birthday of the Prince of Peace, and all come to join in that great refrain . . .

Rejoice, rejoice, Emmanuel . . .
shall come to thee . . . O Israel . . .

—Graham and Dory Hutchins, Arusha, Tanzania.

On Dalla Dallas—Drought and Deluge—and Some Delightful Doings . . . Also Meetings, Markets, Courtrooms, Profiles and Miscellaneous

Greetings . . . We have a lot to tell . . . have been quite busy and off-line a lot due to power shortages. Here is a fun one to brighten your day!

Dalla Dallas: A few years ago in Dar es Salaam, the erstwhile "Capital" of Tanzania, middle-class entrepreneurs began to run mini-busses around the city and charged a fare of five shillings. The five shilling coins were called "dallas" . . . [Probably a takeoff on "dollar"—-and so the small busses were nicknamed "Dalla Dallas."] It stuck—and now all over the country that is their name. They are private contractors who have painted slogans or signs of their choosing on the rear window. We get a real kick out of noticing them.

Here are a few we have seen around Arusha: No Objections—Lollipop—God is Great!—Disinclination—Cobra—High Stepper—Whatever the Case!—Smash!—Unique Sister— Dream Team—Star Wars—Watch Out!—Pick Up da Phone!—Destruction—Get Rich or Die Trying—Golden Eagle—Ruff Cut—Jesus Only!—A Love Situation—All the Way with Jesus—Me Too!—The Best!—Arsenal—Agape—Destruction—Star Wars II—No Kidding—It's not Me its God!—Whatever!

And here is a more serious tale to show how our days are brightening . . . even if it is cloudy . . .

We are *finally* receiving much prayed for rains, and the drought is easing, but too late for some crops, cattle and even the very most vulnerable Africans. Hunger is a major concern and our church, as well as agencies, government and individuals, are all doing what they are able to do to alleviate the suffering. Poverty is everywhere, all the time, but without the rain it becomes more devastating. But God provides in some astonishing ways and the Tanzanian spirit and a friendly and happy outlook on life remains and shines through it all. An old and wise Maasai tells why the wild animals get rain before the rest of us . . . "God gives rain to the wild beasts first, because they don't have any buckets." It is, however, not over, as the shortage of food out in the Maasai lands will not be abated until the newly planted crops can be harvested. Please continue your prayers and gifts on behalf of the hungry.

We have been having power outages here of twelve to fourteen hours duration often, as electric usage is being rationed because of drought all over East Africa. However, thankfully the March rains have come now and this crisis should soon be over as the reservoirs fill up. The other day I was working on the computer on battery and it got dark and I logged off, and then in pitch blackness accidentally knocked my camera off the desk onto the stone tile floor with a great crash. I thought I had broken a set of dishes. The next day, on Sunday I started a photo taking exercise to begin again a photo board for the congregation. My camera did not function properly as I was afraid it wouldn't . . . So today we went downtown to see about getting it fixed, and was sent to the right place we were told it could probably be fixed . . . it is a Nikon and I was afraid I'd have to send it to Japan!

As I came out of the shop Dory was talking with two members of our congregation on the sidewalk. One of them had just returned with her from the epic attempt to climb Mt. Meru and was as sore as Dory was! Then she bought a mango from a woman selling them there and while I waited for her a small boy came up to me begging. I tried to convey to him that I could not give him money . . . [We are warned not to do that here . . . as you can imagine . . . as it encourages begging and some of the "street kids" take the money and sniff glue etc. . . .] So he said to me "banana?" and "lunch?" I told him to wait and when Dory was done we went across the street to where bananas were being sold. Dory then did an amazing thing . . . I just wish I had the video camera handy! She bought a bunch of bananas . . . as the boy suddenly turned into eight to ten boys . . . and more . . . so she began to hand them out to each one . . . Then I noticed she told them to say *asante sana* which is "Thank you!" . . . trying to teach them how to be polite! When she saw that they threw the peelings on the sidewalk they were told by her to pick them up! Which they did! Then one tried to get another banana by hiding the one he had behind his back and she brought his arm forward and said to wait 'till others had one . . . more boys by now had gathered and she bought another bunch of bananas, giving seconds, for after all one banana is not much lunch!

What a sight! What a lady! They were calling her "Mma!" [Which is also what men call grown women here all the time.] "Mma has bananas!" Then we were suddenly surrounded with young men trying to sell us things, and I said . . . "Time to go!" It was an amazing sight! She is fearless, assertive, kind, and incredibly capable and efficient! Then when the bananas were gone . . . one boy wanted her to give him even the stalk from which they were broken. Whether he wanted to eat it or was helping "clean up" . . . we don't know. Hungry kids . . . it nearly breaks your heart. There is a feeding program for street kids, but it is struggling as there are so many. We are glad to feed them but can't let them have cash. The bananas cost 1,000 shillings a bunch = $1.00.

✳   ✳   ✳

This week, we had to go down to the Arusha International Conference Center to pay $261 for our internet services for the coming quarter . . . April–June. The AICC hosts the ICTR—the UN International Criminal Tribunal on Rwanda. Four courtrooms are running five days a week in assessing accountability for the horrible genocide that took place in that country to the northwest of Tanzania in the last decade. While there, we decided to attend some of the hearings, having wanted to do so for some time, but not having the opportunity. It was an awesome and moving experience. We had to present our passports and register to get in so we stayed for the rest of the day and visited three courtrooms. Each was presided over by three judges and the "witness" or the accused was in a screened off area right in front of the glass panel between us, so the public galleries could not see them. They, however got to see us . . . I glanced at the TV in our visitors gallery and suddenly saw . . . us! We were also being filmed!

Attorneys for the prosecution and the defense are at either end of the courtroom. The trials are done in two languages . . . French and English, with translations over the headsets provided. There are also transcripts of hearings done initially before the tribunal in Rwanda in a local dialect available to the court. We have several UN translators, attorneys, and judges in our congregation. In fact, after the second hearing we attended, there was a break for lunch and as we left the visitors gallery and went down the hall, suddenly the judges came through the door and one of them greeted me with, "Reverend! How nice to see you," and explained he wouldn't be in church for three or four weeks as he was returning to his home country of Korea for that time. Later we were greeted by a friend from Cameroon, who is an English-French translator.

The whole UN enterprise here, as you may imagine, is a very impressive and international event done before the eyes and ears of the world. Each panel of judges consists of often three different races, three different nationalities and a mixture of men and women. Likewise, the attorneys are from all over the world, usually bi-lingual at least in English and French, and some more so. This is why Arusha is termed "the Geneva of Africa." Similar courtrooms are in The Hague in the Netherlands, [where their most famous trial has been of Slobodan Milosevic, the "butcher of the Balkans," who recently was found dead in his cell from a heart attack]. If you are interested, you can enter UN ICTR into your search engine on your Internet Explorer and access info regarding the tribunal online.

In one courtroom we heard the prosecutor meticulously refute the previous statements of a witness to the massacres. In the next we heard cross-examination of a witness against a major military officer charged with helping initiate the genocide, and in the third we heard cross-examination of the priest of a parish in Rwanda where in one day 500 or more Tutsis, men, women and children, were forced into hiding in the church by hand grenades and stoning and then when they barricaded themselves in the church it was sprayed with gasoline and set afire. The next day bulldozers were brought in to destroy the church and bury the victims. The witness/priest admitted being there and claiming he was under duress, even to throwing a few stones, but as the cross examination went on, he denied being there at all. It was an incredible thing to witness. If you haven't seen the movie *Hotel Rwanda* . . . by all means get hold of it and watch it. It is indeed a true account, but details only a part of this vast horrendous story of genocide in our time and very near Tanzania.

These trials have been mandated by the UN Security Council to be concluded by 2008. Then, the Darfur ones from the Sudan will need to begin, but some are concerned that they might be held in Europe, which will cost a great deal more. It would also deprive Africa of central responsibility and supervision of that important tribunal.

What we learned from all this is the utmost importance of the rule of law, where the rights of the accused and the accusers are upheld with meticulous respect in discovering what happened and who is responsible for such heinous acts that fill the world with blood. I felt almost like we were at the Nuremberg trials after World War II. What is frightening to many of us today is that our own government is ignoring such important precedents and international laws that have been established regarding acts of war, torture of prisoners, and other treaty obligations under the Geneva Convention, and is deliberately setting aside all that twentieth-century efforts of international cooperation and jurisprudence sought to achieve in order to prevent such catastrophes. But don't get me started! Our current administration has in fact begun World War III under the guise of "The War on Terror" . . . and is succeeding at nothing but bringing disaster upon the world and our nation at an incredible cost in human lives, treasure, and our reputation throughout the world.

✻   ✻   ✻

I was waiting for Graham awhile back to come out of a meeting in a hotel, when I saw a small and thin very old woman wrapped in red and bright yellow sitting at the curbside. Hundreds passed by, looking the other way so as to not see her. A school child noticed and passed, and then looked back again. A businessman with a briefcase stopped and brought out a bill, and gave it to her. A young boy, hands cupped empty to his chest, acknowledged her and his inability to help. A young African woman in slacks and with a shopping bag reached down to give her a coin. Then a woman, carrying a red plastic container on her head, full of tomatoes for sale shared from her meager earnings with the hunched old woman on the sidewalk. I crossed under the low trees to the edge of the deep gutter beside her and said *Bibi* . . . which means "Grandmother" and she turned and leaning toward my outstretched arm with her small aged hand, she nearly toppled into the ditch . . . but caught herself and smiled and bowed her head in thanks. Because we cannot help all . . . do we not help at all? Those who gave out of their little gave the most.

Pentecost, Pangani, Sandals and Surf—Missions and More

Some of you have written wondering about our silence for the past few weeks. We have been quite busy both with the church and with company and have a lot to tell, so we probably had better write it in segments!

Our Service for the Day of Pentecost on June 4th included a brass ensemble, special hymns, and several readers of the lessons revealing the promise and coming of the Holy Spirit. The sanctuary was adorned with red candles, glorious displays of flowers and impressive banners made by Susan, a gifted leader of ACC. Worshippers clothed in garments of different hues of the fire of the Spirit were welcomed as they entered the courtyard by dancing red pennants made by Dory. We printed up a bulletin for the Festival [normally not furnished here] so all the congregants could follow and participate in this important event of the Christian Year, when we celebrate the coming of the Holy Spirit on the Church fifty days after Easter.

After a busy calendar of events in the church, including a Talent Night with an amazing variety of performers and styles of presentation, from musical groups and individuals, to poetry recitations, mime and even comedy! Dory and Graham resurrected a humorous act called "Little Alfie" in which Dory was the hands and Graham was the body and she sought to brush his teeth, wash his face, feed and shave him while hidden behind his back and totally unable to see what was happening. Afterwards, a Tanzanian said he enjoyed it and had never before experienced a pastor acting in such an entertaining and amusing way.

We also had some farewell events for members leaving Tanzania, and then we managed to get away for a mid-week retreat to Pangani on the Indian Ocean. Some friends in the congregation graciously offered us "The Dhow House," a lovely home they have built there.

It was a nine-hour drive to Pangani . . . east through Moshi, and then south past the Eastern Arc Mountains, the Pares and the even more lush and biologically diverse Usambaras. We took a forty-two-kilometer "shortcut" through the bush and a string of villages on a muddy and rutted but passable road. In one village, Graham noticed a crowd of people gathered outside a house. It looked like a meeting taking place. He then noticed that they were all gathered around a large TV watching the World Cup being played in Germany!

We were told to get to Pangani by 6:00 P.M. in order to catch a ferry across the river. We made it at four minutes to 6 only to discover that the state run ferry was disabled and in the local dry dock. Happily there was a "private" ferry that held three cars. We were informed it would be cheaper to wait for two more cars but we were soon able to go with one more and a motorcycle, some bicycles and foot passengers. Arriving on the other side it was getting dark, but with some help from locals walking the road we managed to find our way.

The "Dhow House" is named for the wood from the famous old Arab trader sailing vessels that have plied the East African coast for centuries. They are still a stunning sight with their single sail billowing out as they glide swiftly along the horizon. The wood from the retired dhows is used to adorn houses, with furniture, doors, window and picture frames, banisters and shutters. Over time it develops many small holes and this adds to its charm. We would awake in the morning with light coming through the holes in the shutters. Breakfast on the balcony was a delight, with the sea beckoning us to enjoy the beach and the surf.

This same surf managed to get away with Dory's beautiful new Maasai beaded sandals as the tide came in when we weren't looking. We wandered down the beach searching for them, when she spied a single sole sticking above the sand . . . and lo and behold it was ONE of her sandals! Ah, well . . . she thought . . . I'll wear it with a plain sandal. On returning to the house she told Neema the cook and housekeeper. The next morning came a knock at the door and Neema handed her the *other sandal!* One of the young men who works there found it nearly a mile away on the beach down by the village where he lives! Can you believe it?! We thought it had set sail for India!

For our "retreat" we took along some books to read. We decided we would take this opportunity to read more about Africa. From our church library, located in the new wing, professionally organized and well stocked with donated and mostly used books, Dory chose historical novels [one of her favorite forms of literature] about families that had come

to East Africa to settle and though they endured hardship, personal loss
and tragedy were captivated by the beauty of the land and its people.

Graham found in the church library a biography of David Livingstone. He had for some time wanted to read about this great Scottish
missionary to Africa and read it in one day! He marveled at the fascinating and many sided features of this incredible man. He was very impressive in his Christian conviction and sense of mission, his practice of
medicine and his interest in science . . . [he documented in his journals
very accurately the varied flora and features of the areas in which he
traveled.]

We often hear how Livingstone was a "great explorer" but what is
often forgotten is that this went together with his mission. Some seem
to think his great passion was to find the source of the Nile but are not
sure precisely why. Pushed from the south by the Boers who detested his
mission to the natives, he went into Central Africa and became the first
European to cross the continent, from there to the Atlantic in the west
and to the Indian Ocean on the east. It haunted him that he had not
only opened up Central Africa for missions but had also enabled the
thriving slave trade of the Arabs on the east and the Portuguese on both
coasts. He therefore wanted to find the source of the Nile and facilitate
missions and development to come from the north up the Nile into
Central Africa and help put a stop to the trafficking in human lives and
the practice of slavery. He was a major influence on the British to put an
end to this abomination. Ironically, he offended the London Missionary
Society for his interests in geography . . . they thought it interfered with
missions; and he offended the Royal Geographic Society, who had
awarded him honors and a commission, because he would not give up
his real mission to just become an "explorer"!

One of Livingstone's sons went to look for him in Africa when he
disappeared for a long time after his beloved wife died and was himself
presumed dead, but did not find his father. The son then went to America, arriving there as the Civil War broke out. He joined the Union Army,
and was killed in battle, and is buried at Gettysburg. Father and son . . .
both giving their lives in a fight against slavery. Graham finds it amazing,
that while he was serving a Black church in Cincinnati in 1962 he read
the biography of Abraham Lincoln, and now while in Africa was able to
read the biography of David Livingstone . . . both great emancipators of
a large segment of the human race.

Our delightful time at Pangani came to an end and we returned by the coast via Tanga, the third largest city in Tanzania, and a longer but equally interesting route. We were helped along through Tanga by a hitchhiker we picked up. We then went through a village on the highway where a policeman waved his hand signifying that we should slow down. We did so even though we had already slowed to below the posted speed. When we arrived further down the road to the next town, where the short-cut had taken off, we were hailed to a stop and informed that the policeman in the previous village had really been signaling us to stop. As we hadn't, he now wanted us to wait while he came to where we were. We explained that we had probably misinterpreted his signal and the policewoman got into an argument over the phone and talked him into dropping the matter. She told us to proceed to Arusha as we had been doing, and we arrived home in time to prepare for a breakfast meeting at our house on Saturday morning. More to tell . . . !! But soon! Meanwhile . . . pray for our sad world . . . addicted to violence and war.

—Graham and Dory Hutchins, Angels Always Appearing

The Ferndale Papers

Faith Seeking Understanding

One of the great principles of knowledge of the medieval world was "Faith seeking understanding." This was enunciated in various ways from St. Augustine to St. Thomas Aquinas. It became a very well worked out, elaborated, articulated, and cherished principle both for faith and for knowledge in that civilization. Our modern world seems to have departed from this in many significant ways. With alarming characteristics, at the present time, the field of religion seems to be properly characterized as "Faith avoiding understanding." Often, *we don't really want to know,* but we do *want to believe.* We want a faith that makes us secure, not wise; free from hassle, not an incentive to growth; simple to comprehend, not a great challenge to our thinking. In short: easy, secure, uncomplicated, and quick.

Let us not be fooled by such simplistic approaches to our faith—we
have something *great* to believe in, not something *easy* to believe. The
gospel is simple, yes, but it is not simplistic. It takes study, prayer, discernment, judgment, reflection, growth and a "testing of the spirits, to
see whether or not they are of God." Faith must *seek* understanding, not
merely assume it has it. Let us study to show ourselves approved of God
. . . "rightly dividing the word of truth."

—*The United Church Chimes*, February 1981.

About the Author

Graham Hutchins was born in Boulder, Colorado, and educated at the University of Washington, Boston University and the University of Edinburgh.

He has served congregations in the Church of Scotland, in Ohio, and in the Pacific Northwest Conference of the United Methodist Church at Monitor, Ferndale United, Pullman, and Port Angeles. He has also served in ecumenical, English-speaking international congregations in Jakarta, Indonesia, in La Paz, Bolivia, and most recently in Arusha, Tanzania.

He has taught philosophy, literature, humanities and religious studies in several colleges and universities in Washington and Idaho.

He has published poems in *alive now!*, *The Qumran Anthology*, *Tidepools*, and in various local and ecumenical papers and journals. His book, *Some Words for All Seasons*, available on *Amazon.com*, is an acclaimed series of poems and photographs on the natural and liturgical seasons of the year. He is working on *The Proclamation Project*, an anthology of sermons.

He has won prizes for his photography as well as his poetry, and likes to travel, cook, write, preach, and teach. His wife, Dory, retired from a career in Social Work, shares with him in all the seasons of life and they reside in Port Angeles, when not off serving somewhere else in the world.